Let the Journey Begin

A Parent's Monthly Guide to the College Ex~

Jacqueline Kiernan MacKay
Assistant Vice President, Student Services
Providence College

Wanda Johnson Ingram
Associate Dean of Undergraduate Studies
Providence College

Houghton Mifflin Company   Boston   New York

Director of College Survival: Barbara A. Heinssen
Assistant Editor: Shani B. Fisher
Associate Project Editor: Claudine Bellanton
Editorial Assistant: Christine Skeete
Senior Manufacturing Coordinator: Priscilla Bailey
Marketing Manager: Barbara LeBuhn

Printed in the U.S.A.

ISBN: 0-618-07713-8

23456789-MV-05 04 03 02

To my husband and best friend, Pat MacKay. I am grateful for his constant love, support, and patience and thank him for the endless hours he spent reviewing drafts of the manuscript and for providing much needed tea and sympathy. Most of all, I am grateful for his abiding belief in me.

Since I have written a book for parents, I, of course, want to thank my own mom, Eva Kiernan, for her love and enthusiastic support of my work.

JKM

To my daughter, Keesha, and my mother, Roberta Johnson. I thank my daughter for her love and patience as she began her own journey into the teenage years. I appreciate my mother's never-ending support and inspiration as I juggled home, writing, work, and school. My family has been my greatest source of love and encouragement.

WJI

Contents

Foreword

The first year of college can be an exciting, challenging and even disconcerting experience for both students and their parents. As a parent of three, I experienced this first year phenomenon at three different colleges and by the third time appreciated how each child approached this experience in a unique and very personal way. Since I teach and advise students at a college, I thought I knew everything about the experiences and responsibilities students must confront in their new and sometimes confusing environment. As a parent, however, I learned what it is like to become emotionally involved in my children's trials and successes. This gave me many valuable insights as I later worked with students in the classroom and with their parents in my office.

It has been said that from the time students begin college to when they come home for Christmas break, they will change more than at any other period in their lives. The content of this book places great emphasis on the natural flow of the first-year experience as students change, grow, and mature. As a parent and a professional, I can bear witness to this change and growth. As the authors point out, this book will inform, serve as a resource, and validate your role as parent. It will also be reassuring as you and your student's journey progresses through this "natural flow."

Let the Journey Begin is just what you need to help prepare for what you can expect as you and your child journey through this crucial transitional-period together. Even if you attended college yourself, you will find today's campuses are different in many ways from those in the "dark ages." The unique month-by-month organization of this book provides a description of the events, decisions, and activities that new college students and their parents commonly experience. A list of concerns at the end of each chapter (that is, month) for parents to discuss with their students provides a basis for understanding the issues that might need to be addressed at that particular time. The thoughts and insights of parents and students who have already progressed through this transition will help you anticipate and plan for what may transpire at every stage.

As a resource, this book covers every important facet of the first year of college life and offers you, as a parent, a timely, comprehensive guide to what your child will experience. You might be overwhelmed at first by all the information that is provided. Upon your first reading, skim the contents and then return to specific parts as a month begins or a particular problem arises. Although many of the suggestions and advice given are based on common sense, few resources provide such a practical and organized description of the first year of college. By using this guide, you will be both informed and enlightened as you and your child experience one of life's most important and rewarding journeys.

Virginia N. Gordon, Ph.D.
Assistant Dean Emeritus
The Ohio State University

Introduction

You are probably breathing a big sigh of relief if your child has just completed the process of getting into college. Or perhaps you are shedding a few tears. Whatever you are feeling, you have come to realize that considerable time, energy, and emotions have been spent on the college entrance process. One mom put it this way after leaving her daughter at college for the first time:

> She weaves her way in and out of my life,
> A drifter so she seems.
> Sometimes a child, sometimes a friend,
> Sometimes she's in between.
> It's hard to love and then let go,
> It's hard to hold on, too.
> The time has come to watch afar
> The doors God guides her through.

Letting go is not always easy for parents, and that is perhaps never felt more acutely than the year a child leaves for college. You've spent the past year or so with your child visiting colleges and completing the application and selection process. There were times you provided parental input, and there were times when you encouraged your child to make the decisions. You have shared in the victories and celebrated the good news, and you have comforted during the disappointments.

Now the next stage has arrived. You and your child may have attended college orientation, and you found out what to bring and what to expect. For several weeks, you shopped and packed, and "your student" (which is how the college will refer to your child in letters to you) has just moved into college housing. You are back home now, taking a deep breath, relaxing, and sorting through a variety of different emotions when the telephone rings. It is your child — the college student. The first week of classes has seemed like an eternity, and nothing is going right. Your telephone conversation covers everything from concerns about a noisy roommate to missing all the friends from home. How should you respond? How can you be positive *and* supportive? Suddenly you realize that dropping your child off at college is not the end. Actually your work has just begun. It's time to refocus, switch gears, and prepare to take on the role of a parent of a first-year college student.

Although your student will adjust to college in his or her own unique way, there are still many transitions that all first-year college students face. One of their biggest challenges is being separated from their family and high school friends for the first time. For some students, the process of making friends in a totally new environment is an unsettling experience. Learning how to adjust to the demands of college academic life is another big challenge. Add to this all the new social experiences they face, and you can understand why they are often overwhelmed. As a parent, you too may be experiencing some challenges and some mixed feelings. You might be feeling a sense of pride and excitement for all your child has accomplished. On the other hand, the separation and change can be a bit overwhelming at times. Perhaps you are not sure how you feel sometimes. You might feel confused in your new role, and perhaps this may interfere with your ability to provide support for your child when it is most needed.

College students have a lot of pressure in their first year. They are hoping, they are dreaming, and they are adjusting to a whole new life. They spend a lot of time and energy sorting through their expectations in order to come to terms with the realities of their college experience. At the same time, parents, each in their own way, try to do what is best while struggling with their own transitions and adjustments.

This book is a storehouse of useful information that will give you the necessary tools and ideas to help your son or daughter successfully navigate through the many transitions of college life. You will also understand your own transitions as you make your journey through this first year of college with your child.

Adjustment to college is an ongoing process, and each cycle of the academic year presents its own challenges. Each student's experience is unique, and there is not just one way to respond to particular situations. As a parent, you will need to provide support and encouragement to your child. At the same time, you can assist in fostering your student's growth and independence by giving him or her more and more decision-making responsibility.

This guide for parents will take you on a one-year journey from summer preparations to the end of the first year of college. Chapter 1 begins your journey with the basics: the growth and development issues of college students. It will help you understand the challenges of transition and separation that new students face. It also covers some transition issues unique to specific populations of students: athletes, students of color, students with disabilities, commuter students, and first-generation college students.

Chapter 2 will take you through the orientation experience for students and parents. You will find out about the purpose and expectations of orientation, as well as some strategies designed to help you make the most out of your attendance at parent orientation. Possible questions to ask and issues to address are outlined in detail.

Chapters 3 through 8 take you on a month-by-month excursion through the first year of college. These chapters reinforce the key theme of the book: that adjustment to college is an ongoing process throughout the entire academic year. Each month or cluster of months covers a topic that represents specific challenges during that time. User-friendly features such as parent strategies, commuter sidebars (which provide special advice to commuters), student and parent reflections, and monthly checklists are provided throughout the book.

Be sure to refer to the appendixes at the back of this book. Appendix A is a glossary of terms common to college life. Appendixes B and C provide, respectively, an overview of typical campus resources and helpful web sites for parents.

As you begin to use this book, we suggest that you first read through it completely. This will help you gain a general appreciation for the many complexities of a first-year college experience. You will also be able to see the big picture of the entire year. As the academic year progresses, you can refer back to the chapters that apply to a particular month or segment of the year. You may want to refer to the monthly checklists early on, since they may prompt you to respond in a particular way to a specific issue. Finally, use the space in the margins to write personal notes or list important dates and deadlines.

As professionals who have worked with college students for many years, and especially with first-year students, we have had many opportunities to hear their stories. We have also listened to many of their parents, who try to do what's best. We are especially grateful to them for sharing with us their own first-year transition struggles.

This book will inform you, validate your role as a parent, and serve as a practical resource. It will help you know how to encourage your college student to make the right decisions that will carry him or her successfully through the next four years and beyond. Let the journey begin!

Acknowledgments

We would like to express our appreciation to the many people who contributed to this book in a variety of ways.

We are grateful to the many professionals who provided us with some of their own insights about student-parent first-year adjustment issues. Our thanks go to Brian Bartolini, Eric Bond, O.P., Rose Boyle, Wilesse Comissiong, Sue Costa, Herb D'Arcy, Barbara Fioravanti, Tom Gibson, Sharon Hay, Richie Kless, Kara Kolomitz, Michael Laliberte, Marilyn Miller, Jina Minaya, Maria Montaquila, Geraldine Murphy, and Steven Sears.

A special note of thanks to Ken ("Comma King") Sicard, O.P. our unofficial reviewer, who provided us with valuable advice — sometimes when we did not even ask for it. Our gratitude also goes to Neil Riordan whose expertise greatly assisted us, especially at the beginning of this project.

Our sincere appreciation to Donna Marcone and Natalie Soukatus for their superb organizational assistance and to MaryJane Lenon, Kerri Mercer, Linda Puglia, and Mike Speigler for their technical help.

We thank all those who provided us with their support and enthusiasm over this past year, including Joe Guido, O.P., J. Stuart McPhail, O.P., Mark Nowel, O.P., Ed Caron, and Marifrances McGinn.

We are deeply indebted to the director of College Survival, Barbara Heinssen, and assistant editor Shani Fisher for their support, encouragement, and expert advice. We also thank Sue Vander Hook for her excellent editorial guidance.

The following reviewers who read the manuscript and provided many excellent suggestions for developing this book into its final form deserve special thanks:

Elizabeth Arrison	University of Tennessee at Martin
Kathleen Ragan Fields	University of Wyoming
David M. Fleming	Hope College (Michigan)
Beth Lingren	Southern Illinois University, Carbondale
Jed Liston	University of Montana
Irwin Nussbaum	University of Hartford (Connecticut)
Kimberly Reeve	Wheaton College (Illinois)
Toby R. Shapiro	University at Buffalo (New York)
Judy Spiller	University of New Hampshire
Bill Woodward	Washington University in St. Louis

We express our sincere gratitude to the many students and parents who shared their journeys with us. Their anxieties, their joys, and their struggles are reflected over and over again throughout the book. A special note of thanks to Judy, Ben, and Abbey Sweeney and Ruth Whatmough, Kathy Vermette, and Susan Albert for providing their feedback as the manuscript moved along.

Transitions, Transitions, Transitions

> ❧ *My reactions to my son's leaving for college were as varied as his reactions. I went from encouraging his independence to wanting to wrap my arms around him and tell him he didn't have to go.*
>
> PARENT OF A FIRST-YEAR COLLEGE STUDENT

The transition from high school to college is packed with challenges, excitement, anxieties, and even some surprises along the way. Transitions, for both you and your college student, bring about change, growth, new freedoms, and a new awareness of self and others. They can be unsettling but also serve as a gateway to your student's development as a responsible, mature adult. For the majority of students, the first year of college is a good experience but one that is not without difficulties. It takes time for most students to find their way in their new setting. The more help they have, the easier the transitions will be.

As a parent, part of your transition experience is learning how to respond to issues as they arise. In order for you to do that, you need to be knowledgeable about some of the major transitions your first-year college student will go through. Having an understanding of some basic college adjustment issues will serve as a strong foundation for the year ahead. Now it is time to start your journey, which begins just about at the end of high school.

Going to College for All the Right Reasons

High school graduation is usually a time associated with a flurry of activity: proms, banquets, award ceremonies, parties, and the graduation ceremony itself. It is a time when parents take great pride in their child's accomplishments. It is also a time for parents and students to anticipate the many changes they will encounter over the next year as they embark on their new journey: the college experience.

Over the past year, you and your child probably have been consumed with the dynamics of planning for college: visiting schools, narrowing down choices, filling out applications, and waiting for the decisions. You have shared in the joys, and sometimes the disappointments, of the selection process.

When you are caught up in the excitement of this new venture, you might tend to overlook some of the challenges and choices that your student will face over the course of the next year: deciding on a course of study, adjusting to the demands of college academics, living and learning with others, managing time, communicating needs, and setting personal priorities. How your student approaches these issues depends to a large extent on his or her attitude, maturity, and level of personal and academic skills.

If a student has doubts about attending college or concerns about a college choice, this may interfere with his or her willingness to make meaningful connections with the new campus environment. Although college may seem like a natural progression from high school, not all students make a firm commitment to college. Some go to college because they feel it is expected of them, even though they may have preferred to take a year off after high school. Others reluctantly attend their second or third college choice after the disappointment of not being accepted to their first choice.

The adjustment process can be complicated for students who enter college without resolving these commitment issues. For example, a student who is denied admission to his or her first-choice college may attend another school with the hopes of transferring soon to the first choice. As a result, the student's efforts to become involved with the current institution may be limited. An unwillingness to interact with the campus environment may reinforce the student's negative feelings, which can become particularly harmful if transferring never becomes an option.

Students mature at different rates and bring a variety of coping skills to their situations. Some enter college having already faced some considerable challenges — coping with a learning disability, for example, or dealing with their parents' divorce — and they may have gained some valuable coping skills through these hardships. Others have had very few obstacles up to this point in their lives. They may not have a very large repertoire of coping skills to rely on, and they may have had few opportunities to use their decision-making or problem-solving skills. As a result, a situation that one student manages very easily may seem especially challenging to another.

Personal life skills — managing a budget, banking, doing laundry — can be routine for some students and an entirely new experience for others.

Students with good practical skills have developed a cushion of independence that can make for a smoother transition to college. Students who are doing these activities for the first time, in contrast, may find these practical tasks to be a source of considerable stress. Those who lack these skills may be too embarrassed to ask for assistance.

Every student brings different strengths and weaknesses to the college situation. Some may be well prepared academically for the rigors of college life; others may need considerable assistance with both academic and personal issues. Your student's attitude, maturity level, coping abilities, problem-solving skills, and practical know-how can all serve as a guide for you as you develop realistic expectations for your child's first year of college. Some key strategies will help you see the big picture of your student's experience.

Strategies for Parents

➤➤ Students who are in college for all the wrong reasons may have some unique struggles. Suggest that your student honestly **evaluate the reasons for attending college**. If the college your child is attending is not the number-one choice, encourage him or her to set some short-term goals. Remind your child that making connections is important even if the college is not the first choice. Failing to connect will only result in a self-fulfilling prophecy that "nothing is going right."

➤➤ Attitude can set off emotional responses. Feelings of disappointment, anger, or depression may need to be addressed to help your child cope with a new environment. **Encourage your student to talk** with a counselor or someone at campus ministry to deal with these feelings.

➤➤ Not everyone has had the same life experiences. Encourage your child to learn some **practical skills**, such as managing money and doing laundry, as soon as possible. Gently urge your student to ask for assistance.

Different Colleges — Different Challenges

Attitude, maturity, and academic and personal skills are not the only factors that affect a student's collegiate experience. A variety of other components — the type of institution, its size, its setting, and so on — can present their own set of challenges. Additional factors such as the mission of the institution, its geographical location, and the diversity and gender composition of the student body can have a further impact on the experience.

The size of an institution can affect the number of students per class, the student-faculty ratio, housing options, and the availability of academic programs and college resources. In many cases, a large university has a more diverse population of students, including students of color and those of nontraditional age. Some students may find the atmosphere of a large college or university intimidating; others thrive in such a climate. Some like the idea of being "a small fish in a big ocean," while others insist on being "a big fish in a small pond." Some are attracted to anonymity and a less personal approach; others like a small, intimate atmosphere.

The schedule of the academic year is not the same for all institutions. Although most operate on a two-semester system (fall and spring), some schools are on a quarter system, and a small number have a trimester academic year. A semester is usually about fourteen to sixteen weeks, with a winter break and summer vacation. Quarter systems and trimesters have shorter term sessions, with brief breaks throughout the year. These schedule variations affect a student's vacation time with family and friends, as well as student employment opportunities during the academic year. For example, a student on a quarter system may not get to spend as much time with old friends since the break is shorter or at a different time.

As a parent, you should be aware that all challenges, no matter how small, can be unsettling for a first-year college student. Addressing challenges early can give your student more confidence and enhance self-discovery and adjustment. Your patience, guidance, and empathetic listening will go a long way to help this process along.

First-Year Adjustment

College provides a unique opportunity for parents and the institution to partner together in the development of first-year students. Identifying issues, encouraging the use of support systems, and recommending new strategies are roles for the parent as well as the institution. One common goal is to help students develop their own problem-solving skills rather than to solve their problems or make decisions for them. In order to help your child through this process, you should be aware of some of the important developmental and social themes common to entering college students.

Most experts agree that the first few months of college can present significant challenges for first-year students. One educational researcher indicates that the first six weeks of college are the most critical time in students' adjustment to their new environment. During this period, students need to feel a sense of connection to their institution. Connecting with faculty, staff, advisers, and peers is particularly meaningful during this critical time.

Most colleges and universities have developed a variety of programs and resources to provide opportunities for students to make these connections. First-year-experience programs, mentoring systems, and living and learning programs, which combine academic programs within a residential setting, are examples of some of the more structured approaches. Residence life staff also play an important role in helping students make meaningful associations with peers, faculty, and others. At most colleges, social and educational programs are regularly sponsored during the evening in the residence halls. For commuters, many colleges also provide special facilities and services such as lounges, newsletters, and clubs.

The awareness of another important concept that students learn by becoming involved can further assist parents in understanding the many complexities of the college experience. According to a leading expert on student development, the more students become involved in their college experience, the more likely they are to succeed.[1] Involvement can happen at many levels. It might be the number of hours invested in study outside the classroom or time spent at an on-campus work-study job. Your student might become involved in community service, become a member of a college club or organization, or spend extra hours in campus ministries.

> *Believe it or not, having something other than school actually improved my grades. It made me focus more on time management, and I knew that I had limited time to get work done, so if I wanted to be involved with a club or a sport, I needed to use my free time to do work. I like being involved with the pastoral service organization because we had meetings every week and I felt like I had a lot in common with the students I met.*
>
> STUDENT REFLECTION

Whatever your child's involvement, it is important for both of you to know the difference between becoming involved on campus and interacting socially. Participating in a flurry of social activities does not require the kind of commitment and investment to a new college environment that will enhance the learning process. For example, a student who chooses to party three nights a week may be involved socially, but that involvement may be counterproductive to the learning process. On the other hand, a student who becomes involved in a campus organization shares common interests and goals with other students, works with peers on various levels,

[1] Astin, A.W. "Student Involvement: A Developmental Theory for Higher Education," *Journal of College Student Personnel*, 1984, 25, 297–308.

and probably develops leadership skills and meaningful relationships. Remember to encourage your child to get involved in campus activities that will enhance the college experience.

New students view their world from extremes: right or wrong, good or bad, beautiful or ugly.[2] During this time, they look to authority figures as the experts to provide the "one right answer." They may look to professors, advisers, or deans for answers to all their college-related questions instead of relying on their own decision-making skills. For example, a student who enters college with an undeclared major may become frustrated with an adviser who suggests various course options but does not state exactly what courses to take. Because the student is anxious about making a wrong decision and believes the adviser should have all the answers, he or she may avoid decision-making responsibility.

Understanding your child's development, growth, and independence will help you validate and support your child's decisions. It can help you to see the bigger picture when addressing everyday adjustment issues. It can also provide you with an appreciation for the many resources that colleges have developed to assist students in their first-year journey.

First-Year-Experience Programs

Many colleges and universities have structured programs and courses specifically designed to assist first-year students with basic transition issues. A goal of many of these programs is to extend the orientation process into the academic year. Some of these programs have a strong academic component, some focus more on social and personal adjustment issues, and others offer a blend of both. Many offer academic credit and may even involve residential life in an attempt to link academic and nonacademic issues. The majority of these programs are voluntary, although some require the participation of all new students.

These programs, largely modeled after the University of South Carolina's "University 101" course which extends orientation throughout the first year, are designed to help students feel a connection between themselves and the institution early in their academic career. Small group seminars, involvement with faculty outside the classroom setting, and group participation in social and cultural events all work to achieve this goal. In some instances, the seminar leader also serves as the student's academic adviser.

[2] Perry, W.G., Jr. *Forms of Intellectual and Ethical Development in College.* New York: Holt, Rinehart & Winston, 1970.

In the beginning I wasn't sure that I had made the right decision about joining a freshman program. But it turned out to be just what I needed. Because my classes were small, I really got to know some of the students pretty well. Also, it was great to be able to get off campus once in a while. We went to a jazz concert and made two trips to museums during the first semester. We even had dinner at my professor's house a couple of times. This made my fine arts requirement much more enjoyable, rather than sitting in class and just listening to lectures.

STUDENT REFLECTION

Some colleges provide an opportunity for students to fulfill a core requirement through involvement in a first-year-experience program. For example, a college that requires six credits in humanities may designate some sections as first-year-experience courses. Students enrolled in these courses typically meet three times a week in class and one evening a week in an informal seminar. While the classroom experience focuses on academics, the evening seminar addresses basic adjustment issues such as time management, healthy lifestyles, and substance abuse. In well-developed seminar programs, the students sometimes live in the same residential hall and even attend off-campus performances together as part of their course requirement.

In these programs, students and faculty connect both inside and outside the classroom. Faculty involvement outside class might include attending cultural events with students, sponsoring an informal dinner in the residence hall, or conducting an evening seminar within the student's living environment. These kinds of activities can go a long way in breaking down barriers between faculty and entering students.

Because the number of students in each class is limited, there are many informal, interactive exchanges between students and faculty. Small group seminars, in contrast to large lectures, provide an opportunity for students to advance their oral communication skills and develop meaningful relationships with their peers. Small classes also provide first-year students with the opportunity to fit in and become part of a community focused on learning rather than recreation.

Although there are many advantages to first-year-experience programs, they may not be the best fit for all students. Some may find the programs too limiting and too structured. Other students might be intimidated by the smaller class size and feel uncomfortable engaging in small group discussions. Some students may need a more diversified experience.

Your student needs to do some "homework" before getting involved in a first-year program. Most programs publish brochures that provide information about the courses, out-of-class activities, and requirements for admission. Students should consider calling or meeting with the program director to gather more information or to answer any questions or address concerns. Because of the kind of commitment a student must make to a first-year-experience program, your student should make the final decision about getting involved. Although you may find the program attractive, pushing your child to participate against his or her will can only complicate the adjustment process.

Transitions for Specific Populations

The transition from high school to college can be a complex process. Some students may experience additional pressures because of who they are and what they bring to their new setting. These students — students with disabilities, student athletes, commuters, first-generation college students, students of color, and others — often require different choices and options.

Not all students fit neatly into a specific category. Although all have common issues, some specific populations should know how their issues are different and how the college can help. It is important that all students know their choices and options while not feeling labeled or stereotyped in any way. Parents of students within these specific populations can play a vital role in providing the necessary information and support during the adjustment period of the first year of college. Some important transition issues that can complicate the adjustment process for these students are described below. Also mentioned are some general services and resources that colleges provide to assist a variety of student populations.

Students with Disabilities Colleges are required by federal law to follow the mandates of Section 504 of the Rehabilitation Act (Section 504, 1973) and the Americans with Disabilities Act (1990) in providing equal access and reasonable accommodations to students with disabilities. The statute under Section 504 states, "No otherwise qualified handicapped individual, shall solely by reason of his/her handicap, be excluded from participation in, be denied the benefits of, or be subjected to discrimination under any program or activity receiving federal financial assistance."

Different disabilities call for different accommodations. For instance, a student with attention deficit disorder may require extended testing time, alternate test settings, or note-taking services. A student with a physical disability may need special physical accommodations in order to live on campus. Ramps, key entry systems, close proximity to exits and elevators, and placement on a lower-level floor of a residence hall are some of the accessibility factors that may need to be planned.

Most colleges have someone who coordinates services for students with disabilities. It is important that parents and students understand the institution's policies and procedures when requesting services and accommodations. Students must first let the college know that they have a disability before the college can respond in an appropriate manner. Then they need to provide the official documentation necessary — for example, psychoeducational testing, medical documents, or clinical reports — to verify the disability. The more specific the documentation is, the better the college will be able to provide assistance. Once the appropriate personnel review the documentation, the college will make a plan that will best provide for the student's needs.

Students with disabilities may encounter some significant — and unsettling — differences between high school and college. For example, they may miss the central resource room in their high school that allowed them to network with other students who had similar issues and required similar accommodations. This resource room also provided a much-needed additional support system.

Also remember that in college, it is the student, not the parent, who must take an active role in talking, disclosing, and petitioning about issues related to the disability. Some students may find it difficult to adjust to this new role as self-advocate. Also, a student who is afraid that other students will know about his or her disability may be hesitant to disclose important information to the appropriate adviser, faculty member, or resource coordinator.

Students with disabilities may experience some additional stress if they feel that their disability is interfering with their efforts to fit in and be accepted by their peers. In some cases, they may be reluctant to get involved in social activities. Of course, this usually depends on the nature of the disability and the student's capacity to cope and seek assistance when necessary.

In order to deal with these many challenges and the added stress, students with disabilities need to be aware of the assistance and interventions that colleges offer. Some schools have formal programs, while others have less structured systems. Counseling, support groups, and assistance in learning self-advocacy skills are some of the services students should explore. These resources provide a community base of support that helps to strengthen a student's problem-solving skills. Early in the first semester, students should work toward developing a relationship with the individual or office that is responsible for coordinating services for students with disabilities.

Parents of a college student with a disability may have to make some unique adjustments of their own during that first year. The process of letting go may be more difficult for these parents. For the first time, they may have to play a less active role in advocating for the needs of their student. Now they may need to pull back and let their student advocate on his or her own behalf.

Parents need to keep in mind a number of issues as their student with a disability makes the transition from high school to college. In high school, parental involvement was mandatory. In college, the responsibility for decision making falls on the student. The parent can play an indirect role by providing support and direction and by discussing expectations and exploring ways to help the process move along. Neither the parent nor the student should expect the college to meet every one of their wants and desires, but they should expect reasonable accommodations for documented needs. Their request and the resulting accommodation should be reasonable and relevant to the disability.

Student Athletes Another special population that may face unique issues is the student athlete. High school athletic programs are different from college programs, and adjustments are necessary. There are many positive benefits to being a college athlete. Athletes tend to develop a sense of teamwork, fine-tune their physical and mental skills, participate in an activity that satisfies a passion and contributes to a sense of pride, and become part of a peer group of students who share a similar goal. However, the double role of being a student and an athlete brings with it both advantages and added responsibilities.

Juggling academics with training, practice sessions, and competition can sometimes seem like an overwhelming task for a first-year college athlete. Many college athletes assume that because they successfully handled these tasks in high school, they will fall into a similar routine in college. This may be the case for some students, but many will discover that they must have much more self-discipline to set firm priorities and learn good time management skills.

Some student athletes may be surprised to find that the level of physical workouts and practices is more intense in college than in high school. This can contribute to increased fatigue, weight loss or gain, overall wellness issues, and academic decline. Attending class, participating in classroom discussions, and preparing for a test all require energy, concentration, and motivation. Athletes often have to "psych themselves up" for a game and prepare for an exam on the same day.

Travel obligations can also affect a student athlete in a number of ways. Developing a plan to make up work and tests from missed classes can be a challenge for even the most experienced student. It is important that student athletes not assume that "everything will be taken care of." They should become aware of their institution's policy for notifying faculty about team travel schedules. They also need to know their own role and responsibility to complete assignments.

Parents and students also should know how the college addresses the needs of student athletes. Being knowledgeable of academic support systems is imperative to this process. Usually during the recruiting period, student athletes and parents have an opportunity to meet personally with the coach or a member of the coaching staff. At this time, parents should be prepared to ask questions about the role of the academic adviser, the expectations of the faculty, and the availability of tutorial services. Students and parents should also ask about eligibility and scholarship requirements. Orientation for new students will help athletes to see themselves as members of the entire college community rather than only members of an athletic team.

Parents and athletes should also be aware of nonacademic issues that may affect how a first-year student athlete adjusts to college. For example, most students make important campus connections through extracurricular activities, residential living, and time spent on campus interacting with peers. Because student athletes spend so much time in their sport and with their teammates, they may become isolated from the rest of their campus community. Student athletes and their parents need to ask questions about housing for athletes (*Do they live together, or are they integrated through the campus?*) and questions about support systems (*Are mentoring and orientation programs available for athletes?*). It is important for athletes and their parents to know how the college views the role of the student athlete, both inside and outside the classroom.

Parents should pay particular attention to their student athlete during the off-season. Some students find it difficult to adjust to less structure and less involvement with teammates during the off-season. This can affect their motivation and their morale for their entire college experience. On the other hand, off-season is a time when many athletes are expected to be involved in strenuous conditioning programs that require a readjustment of their time and energy.

Parents of student athletes will need to make some personal transitions and adjustments during this first year. When their child was in high school, the parents may have been accustomed to attending sporting events regularly and sharing in their child's victories and defeats. Then they may have become very involved in the college recruiting process at many different levels. After investing so much of themselves into the world of their student athlete, parents may now feel somewhat isolated and out of touch with their child's experiences. These feelings may be magnified when the team is required to travel during the holidays or school breaks, and their student athlete is unable to come home. For parents who live far from the college, not being able to attend games or meets can make them feel even more removed from their child's life.

When you are aware of these transition issues, you and your student will be better prepared for them, and you will have more realistic expectations. Parents will realize that communication may not always be what they hope for. Their student's time demands for academics, practice, games, and travel will reduce a parent's involvement. Be sure you discuss feelings and expectations with your student. You may want to establish a designated weekly time for a telephone call. This way, you can stay involved and provide the appropriate support for your student athlete.

Commuter Students Many colleges find it particularly challenging to assist commuter students with their first-year adjustment to college. Their needs are varied since some commute by choice and others because of financial restrictions or family obligations. The ease of the transition may also depend on the nature of the institution, that is, whether it is predominantly residential or commuter. For the commuter who spends a limited time on campus, making connections often can be a real struggle.

Students who live in a residence hall have regular opportunities to connect with their peers. Roommates and floormates share everyday common living experiences that help break down social barriers early in the academic year. Commuters have to work harder to develop relationships with their peers. They need to make a conscious effort to attend events and programs that will allow them to meet other students. Some may find this difficult because of family, work, and other obligations. Others may be less enthusiastic and motivated to develop new relationships because they are comfortable with their current friendships from high school.

Many commuter students are reluctant to make use of campus resources because they think that they are designed for resident students. Parents can play an important role by encouraging their commuter student to connect with college services such as counseling, advising, and student health. Although a student may live in the community where the college is located, attendance at orientation is still important since it provides with the opportunity to connect with the campus and meet new people. It is also important for a commuter student to explore the special programs and resources designed specifically for them. Newsletters, web sites, clubs, and organizations with the commuter in mind can provide a necessary link between the student and the college. Some colleges have commuter lounges — a good place for new students to meet other commuters. Lounges

Commuter Students

also provide students with a space of their own, especially when there are large blocks of time between classes. Many schools also have a designated individual or office to coordinate services for commuter students such as parking facilities, carpooling, or safety and security issues. Social activities are also coordinated to encourage students to connect with their campus. Each of these services will help commuters to feel more like insiders.

From the very beginning of the year, it is important for commuter students and their parents to discuss their expectations of the college experience and how this experience will differ from high school. Some of these differences include blocks of time between classes, a more demanding academic program, and evening commitments. These differences require students and parents to do some problem solving in order to navigate through this environment. Responding to your student as if he or she were still in high school with the same expectations for family obligations will probably be counterproductive. At this stage in your child's education, you need to foster his or her independence and autonomy. Your role may be merely to adjust to your child's changing schedule and make room in the house for a regular study area. These approaches will ease your student into a smooth transition from high school to college.

First-Generation College Students First-generation college students face some unique challenges as they approach their college years. Being the first member of their immediate family to attend college can be a source of tremendous pride, but it can also bring along with it some unexpected burdens. The pressure to succeed academically may be coupled with the fear of failure and the anxiety of living up to family expectations.

The desire to succeed and even pave the way for siblings and other family members can sometimes produce unrealistic pressures to excel and even interfere with a student's ability to do well. For example, in an effort to be successful, a first-generation college student may focus all of his or her attention on studying and fail to take advantage of important social and personal outlets. Parents who may be unfamiliar with college life will probably sense that things are not going well but may not know how to help.

For many students in this population, one of the major obstacles to overcome is their parents' limited understanding of the collegiate experience. Since the high school years serve as their only frame of reference, parents are often unaware of the significant differences between high school and college. The intensity of academic programs, the time commitments, and the increased need for independence may be underestimated and misunderstood by parents of first-generation college students. Although they may take immense pleasure in their child's accomplishments, they may not always know when to provide appropriate encouragement and support.

First-Generation College Students

They have no repertoire of memories of their own college experience to fall back on.

Not being familiar with college life may cause some parents to develop unrealistic expectations. For example, parents may assume that the student who lives on campus will travel home every weekend. A student who travels home often may do so because he or she feels guilty about "deserting the family" and, as a result, may forgo some important on-campus connections.

Some parents may be confused about their student's choice of academic major. For parents and students, there is a general tendency to connect a major with a specific career. For example, a student who chooses to major in history rather than something like accounting may be questioned about the practicality of such a decision.

It is important for parents of first-generation college students to learn as much as they can about the college experience. Attending college family day programs and admissions seminars will help them gain general information. Parent orientation programs are especially useful for information about academic and nonacademic issues. These programs can help parents sift through the realities and sort out their expectations concerning the college experience. At the same time, they will find out about important campus services and resources. Parent organizations or councils can also help parents stay informed about current issues and trends at their child's institution.

Students of Color Students of color bring to their campus a rich blend of racial, ethnic, and cultural diversity. How they respond and interact in their new college environment often depends on a number of factors: the campus climate, the amount of diversity in the student-faculty population, and the student's own sense of identity. These factors play an important role in a student's successful transition from high school to college.

The nature of the college and what it has to offer students of color will have a considerable impact on these students. Predominantly white colleges, historically black colleges and universities, rural colleges, urban institutions, and church-affiliated colleges all have their own unique climate which can be perceived as welcoming and inclusive, or indifferent and exclusive. Each individual's perception can affect how well he or she copes in the new environment.

Some of the college challenges that students of color may face include feelings of isolation due to a lack of institutional diversity, very few cultural opportunities, differences in food preferences, meaningful role models, and institutional racism. Because of the amount of time students spend in their campus living environment, residential life can sometimes be the focus of misunderstandings and mixed messages. In the classroom, students of color may find themselves dealing with verbal and nonverbal behaviors that can interfere with their learning process. Various aspects of the curriculum, such as course content and presentation of the material, can also affect a student's relationship with the college. For example, when discussing the topic of affirmative action, a professor might turn to the only student of color in the class to give an "expert answer."

How a student addresses these issues can be critical to his or her overall college adjustment. Allowing situations and emotions to build up may create a residue of negative feelings that can complicate the transition process. It is important for students of color to connect with one or two individuals with whom they feel comfortable, relying on them for support and advice. Creating a strong support network early on can help students to develop a possible course of action and help serve to model assertive communication skills. A student who is experiencing problems with on-campus living should seek out a residence life staff member as soon as possible. These trained individuals can help a student assess a problem, generate options, and work out misunderstandings. Also, students may want to talk with upper-class students of color who can share how they addressed similar experiences and help the student put the problem in perspective.

It is important for all students to participate in activities and programs that interest them, such as student government, community service, clubs, and organizations, in order to make important campus connections. Students of color may want to get involved in cultural activities, heritage festivals, and multicultural programs that help them celebrate their own cultural identity and uniqueness. Seeking out and attending cultural events and activities within the local community is an effective way for all students to supplement their college's on-campus programs.

Students of color can take a proactive approach in dealing with potential problems by understanding what they bring to their college environment, by communicating the nature of their own unique needs, and by having a sense of what obstacles they may have to overcome. Parents can be especially helpful in brainstorming possible strategies and encouraging open communication as issues arise.

Attendance at orientation programs can help parents and students learn about the institution and identify vital campus resources. It is important for all students (and particularly students of color) to identify early the support systems — mentoring programs, support groups, leadership groups, multicultural centers — that can help ease their transition to college and provide a community base of support.

If and when concerns arise, parents and students need to know the appropriate channels of response. Deans of multicultural affairs, affirmative action officers, and campus ombudsmen are just some of the individuals specially trained to deal with problems. Student handbooks contain important information about college policies and procedures and usually give details on how and where to file grievances. Finally, although these issues may be emotionally charged, it is important for parents to keep in mind that it is the student who must take on the responsibility for addressing issues in an appropriate manner.

Other Populations There are other groups of students whose transition to college may be complex because of unique issues they bring with them. As a result, these students may come to their new setting with a different perspective on first-year issues.

Transfer students may approach their new institution with a variety of emotions. Some may look forward to a new beginning, while others may still be dealing with leftover baggage from their previous college experience. Students of a different sexual orientation might look for others to identify with in their new setting. Women may encounter gender barriers such as sexist language, sexual harassment, and lack of support for career goals. International students face a dual adjustment — adjusting to a new college experience and a new culture.

Whatever issue or special need a student brings to the first year of college, there is usually a person, a resource, a publication, a support group, a club, or an organization that can provide assistance. The proper connection can make the transition process less stressful and more positive for first-year students.

Orientation FAQs (Frequently Asked Questions)

🐌 *At the close of orientation, I was sitting next to the bookstore waiting for my son to complete registration. A family clearly touring the campus for the first time came down the stairs looking bewildered and on overload. I remember I felt exactly that way when we toured. Now, sitting there, I felt at ease, ready and confident that our son was as well prepared as possible to begin the year. I credit these feelings to the orientation team and the way they anticipated and addressed issues for my son and myself, which helped to demystify the experience.*

PARENT OF A FIRST-YEAR COLLEGE STUDENT

Most colleges and universities offer an orientation program for incoming students, the first step in an ongoing adjustment process. Orientation bridges the gap between the expectations of a college experience and the reality of the first year. Whether or not attendance is mandatory, you would do well to take advantage of this opportunity.

Many colleges have formal orientation programs for parents as well. In fact, some institutions sponsor overnight programs for students and their parents. These programs can be held as early as mid-June or just before classes begin in the fall.

The goal of orientation is to introduce students and their parents to the college — its programs, academic and nonacademic resources, policies and procedures — and issues related to college life. It also provides an opportunity for students to meet faculty, key college personnel, and other students. The format may include seminars, skits, workshops, informal social events, slide shows, panel presentations, and outdoor experiences.

Orientation

17

The topics covered at orientation vary from school to school, but there are some common elements. Most student orientation programs cover academic advising, placement exams, academic requirements, health and wellness issues, campus tours, housing and roommate selection, and student life and activities. At many schools orientation is also a time when students register for fall semester classes. Parent orientation usually includes many of these same components, but may also address such issues as parent expectations, financial aid and billing, and how to help your child adjust to college. Some schools also involve members of parent councils or alumni. You will probably go home with a huge collection of materials for both you and your student to review.

No matter how thorough and interesting the orientation program is, some students come away with more negative than positive feelings. Many approach orientation with unrealistic expectations, hoping to make instant friends and become comfortable with the college during this short time. Others are overwhelmed with the confusing aspects of the course registration process. These feelings might reinforce some of the self-doubts they had earlier in the summer about their choice of college. Don't panic; these reactions are normal. Once again, good parent-child communication is the key. Take some time to reinforce your student's decision-making skills.

> 🐌 *I was really anxious about orientation because I didn't know what to expect. My parents told me to relax, enjoy the time, and keep an open mind. As a result, I probably got more out of it than most of my friends.*
>
> STUDENT REFLECTION

Questions to Ask at Orientation

Information about college policies, procedures, and services can usually be found in a number of sources. The student handbook and the college bulletin are two important publications that students and parents should become familiar with. In addition, some departments distribute their own publications such as a residence life manual, a student health booklet, or a guide for first-year students. Many colleges also have handbooks for parents of entering students. Much of this information is often available on the college's web site.

The remainder of this chapter is devoted to frequently asked questions (FAQs) at orientation. The questions are grouped by subject to help you navigate through the wide array of possible questions. Knowing what to ask will help you maximize the benefits of your orientation experience.

My Child's Records

Many parents of college students are surprised to learn that they may not have the same access to information about their child, such as grades, class attendance, and so forth, that they had in high school. Federal legislation has mandated policies and procedures that colleges must follow.

The Family Educational Rights and Privacy Act of 1974 (FERPA), also known as the Buckley Amendment, was designed "to assure parents of students, and students themselves if they are over the age of eighteen or attending an institution of post-secondary education, access to their education records and to protect such individuals' rights to privacy by limiting the transferability [and disclosure] of their records without their consent" (*Congressional Record*, 1974, p. 39862). In other words, the rights of parents transfer to the student unless the college decides to give parents access to the records. Colleges have varying policies when it comes to parental access to information.

Frequently Asked Questions

Who has access to my child's grades? (deans? faculty? advisers? coaches? parents?) Does my child have to sign a release form to allow someone access to grades?

Will I be notified if my child needs counseling or treatment from student health services? from emergency services?

Who has access to my child's judicial or disciplinary records? (faculty? advisers? coaches? parents? employers? postgraduate institutions?)

Academic Policies and Procedures

Most institutions publish academic information such as degree requirements, academic policies, course descriptions, and an academic calendar in a document usually known as the college bulletin or college catalogue. It is very important for students to understand academic policies since they are ultimately responsible for fulfilling all the requirements for graduation.

Frequently Asked Questions

What are the basic academic policies of the college?
- What are the attendance policies?
- What is the typical course load?
- What are the grade requirements?
- What are the dismissal and probation policies?
- What are the qualifications to get on the dean's list?
- How does the college handle transfer credits?
- How does a student add or drop a course?
- What is the policy on absences due to illness or emergencies?

What are the core (general) requirements expected of all students? (number of credits? number of courses? specific disciplines? advanced placement credits? College Level Examination Program?)

What are the requirements of a specific major or minor?
- What courses are required?
- What are the prerequisites?
- What are the required total number of credits?
- What exploratory courses are available?

What are the options for students who enter without a major?

How do students register for courses? (on the web site? by telephone? in person? through an academic adviser?)

How will my child be advised to take the appropriate courses? (by a faculty adviser? by a peer adviser? at the advising center?)

What types of enrichment programs are available? (study abroad? internships? summer programs? intersessions? distance learning? first-year student programs?)

What facilities are available to assist students in research activities? (library? computer labs? on-line databases?)

What assistance is available to students experiencing academic difficulty or who may have special needs? (tutorial programs? academic resource center? learning specialist? testing services? disability services?)

Residence Life

If your child will be living on campus, there is some very general and practical information that you and your student should be aware of before moving in. When a college assigns roommates, it usually asks students to complete a questionnaire that indicates personal habits, likes, and dislikes. There are some other questions you may want to ask too.

Frequently Asked Questions

What is the composition of the residence halls? (single sex? coed? singles? doubles? triples? quads? suites? theme-related halls, i.e., substance free, honors, first-year-experience?)

How are students assigned to the halls? (random selection? student preference?)

How are roommates assigned? (random assignments? matched according to personal preference?)

When are students informed about their roommate assignments?

Is smoking allowed in rooms or residence halls?

In addition to a bed and desk, what furnishings will be provided? What should students bring? (lamps? hangers? linens? iron? ironing board? rug?)

What appliances are allowed? (refrigerator? microwave? television?)

Is there cable availability in the rooms?

What laundry facilities are available? Is there a linen service? What are the costs?

Are storage facilities available during semester break? (on campus? off-campus rentals? lockers?)

How are telephone services provided? (telephone rentals? voice mail? long-distance systems? phone bills?)

What do students need to know to have a computer in their room? (hard wiring? networking? surge protectors? security cable? software? insurance coverage?)

What are the safety and security measures in the residence halls? (room security? hall security? campus escort? shuttle service? emergency telephones? fire alarms? smoking in rooms? sprinkler systems? state-mandated fire drills?)

What meal plan options are available? (five-day plan? seven-day plan? credits?)

Is housing available during semester breaks when classes are not in session?

What are the food arrangements during breaks?

What are the accommodations for athletes during the break?

What security measures are in place during break?

Are there any additional charges for staying on campus during breaks?

How are special needs accommodated? (hearing or sight impaired? wheelchair access? learning disabilities? special diets? allergies?)

Health and Counseling Services

Counseling centers and student health centers are maintained on most college campuses. The services that these resources provide vary greatly. For the most part, the larger the school is, the more extensive these services are. There are usually more services if the campus is primarily residential and if it is affiliated with a medical school. Smaller commuter schools often have limited on-campus services and may even contract out with local clinics or hospitals to provide health and counseling services for students.

Frequently Asked Questions

What are the hours of the health center? Are facilities available to keep students overnight? (day, evening, weekend hours? options if facility is not open twenty-four hours?)

How is the health center staffed? (full time? part time? physicians? nurses? physician assistants? nutritionist? health educator?)

Are there separate costs for the use of health services? (annual fee? fee-for-services? emergency billing?)

What services are available on campus, and when are referrals made off-campus? (x-rays? prescriptions? lab tests? allergy shots? birth-control information? OB-GYN services? treatment for major illnesses? emergencies?)

How are special or chronic health needs handled? (daily medication? injections? regular lab testing?)

Will I be contacted if my child requires emergency treatment? (school policy? hospital policy? treatment of a minor? insurance information?)

Does the college have mandatory health insurance? (plans? options available? cost?)

What kinds of counseling services are provided? (short-term? long-term? psychological testing? support groups?)

How are after-hour emergency counseling situations handled? (crisis intervention? counselor on call?)

What are some typical issues that a student may bring up with a counselor? (substance abuse? eating disorder? depression? sexual assault? family crisis? test anxiety?)

How does the college educate students about alcohol and drug use or abuse? (residence hall programs? newsletters? peer education? health educator? seminars?)

Are there specific services and resources available for alcohol and drug abuse? (substance abuse counselor? support groups? Alcoholics Anonymous meetings? off-campus resources?)

What counseling staff is available? Is there a fee for use of services? (clinicians? consultants? peer counselors? referral to private clinicians? agencies?)

Career Services

Most career service offices provide a wide range of resources to students of all years and all majors. For seniors, services focus on their postgraduate plans and range from conducting a job search to developing effective interview skills. Undergraduates can benefit from these services early on by taking advantage of interest testing, self-assessment tools, and internships.

Frequently Asked Questions

How does the college help students choose a major? (self-assessment? Computer-assisted programs? group work? adviser? career counselor?)

What type of assistance is available to students once they have chosen a major? (career library? resumé and interview skill building? alumni career network? on-campus recruiting?)

What kinds of internships are available? (academic credit? volunteer? paid? summer experience?)

How can students find information about jobs available for seniors graduating with specific majors? (academic department statistics? career office report? alumni newsletter?)

What assistance is available for students interested in attending graduate school? (faculty adviser? graduate exam preparation? information on graduate school listings and financial aid?)

Student Life Policies and Procedures

In order to provide an atmosphere conducive to learning and respectful of individual rights, colleges have clear policies that are enforced by specific offices and individuals. Although systems may vary depending on the size and mission of the institution, there are a number of issues, such as alcohol and drug use and abuse, safety and security, and disciplinary procedures, that are common to all colleges. It is important for students to be aware of the college regulations, which are typically set out in the official student handbook.

Frequently Asked Questions

What are the college's policies concerning alcohol and drug use and abuse? (under-age drinking? serving minors? use and distribution of illicit drugs?)

How does the college enforce its alcohol and drug policies? (residence hall supervision? monitoring of on-campus events? overseeing activities of sororities, fraternities, and athletic events?)

What other campus policies exist concerning student behaviors? (hazing? gambling? vandalism? theft? physical and sexual assault? motor vehicle violations?)

What procedures are in place for students who violate campus policies? (formal discipline process? informal review? peer mediation?)

What are the sanctions imposed on a student who violates campus policies? (fines? educational programs? community service? probation? suspension? expulsion?)

If a student is found guilty of a violation, who is notified? (depends on level of severity of offense? parent notification? police notification? registrar's office notification?)

What is the college's policy concerning students having a car on campus? (first-year student restrictions? parking stickers or decals? hang tags? parking fees? accommodations for special needs?)

What measures are in place to provide for the safety and security of students? (lighting? fire drills? emergency telephones? campus escort service? shuttles? parking facilities? security video monitors? security or police force?)

What assistance is available for a student who is a victim of a crime? (police? counseling? sexual assault administrator? campus safety officer? emergency health services? rape crisis? emergency hot line?)

Where can I find information on campus crime statistics as mandated by federal law? (security office? student services or affairs? public information office? published material?)

Finances and Student Spending

By the time orientation arrives, most families that have applied for financial aid have received an award letter identifying their student's aid package. However, you still may have questions about some specific issues such as typical student expenses and money management concerns.

Frequently Asked Questions

How does a specific financial aid package affect tuition payments? (grants? loans? scholarships? merit awards? work-study? monthly payment plans?)

Are loans and scholarships renewable each year? If so, what is the process? (dates and deadlines for renewal? grade point average renewal requirements? application forms? Free Application for Federal Student Aid [FAFSA]?)

How is a work-study program implemented? (job listings? payment? hours? supervision?)

What resources are available to help students get a non-work-study position? (student employment office? job listings? co-op opportunities? clearinghouse resources?)

What are some typical costs for first-year students? (textbooks? supplies? entertainment? transportation? spending money?)

What banking options are available? Are there special campus systems in place for students? (smart cards? debit cards? credit cards? ATM machines? banking and check cashing facilities? student discounts for banking services?)

Miscellaneous Matters

There may be additional information you want to seek that does not fall into any of the previously mentioned categories. Some of the questions below may be helpful to you.

Frequently Asked Questions

What additional resources and support systems are available to students? (campus ministry? learning assistance center? multicultural affairs? athletic adviser?)

Are there special services for commuter students? (commuter lounge? commuter organizations? programs? newsletter? lockers? adviser? parking?)

What kinds of activities are available for students who wish to get involved in campus activities? (clubs? organizations? sporting events? cultural programs? leadership development? student government? Greek letter organizations? multicultural affairs? campus ministries? campus service opportunities?)

How can students find out information about activities, clubs, and organizations? (student union? student association? club offices and bulletin boards? newsletters? campus newspaper? web sites?)

How can a student supplement his or her program with fine arts and cultural programs? (dance? music? music lessons? theater? acting? performances?)

What athletic activities are available for students? (varsity sports? intramural programs? club sports? recreational center? fitness programs?)

What personal services are available to students on campus? (post office? computer, copy, fax service? florist? dry cleaning? restaurants? hair salon? video rentals?)

Where can parents and students find a list of important dates and deadlines? (newsletters? academic calendar? college bulletin? web site? student handbook? parent handbook?)

What special programs and resources are available to parents of first-year students? (parent organizations or councils? newsletters? special family weekends? hotel and transportation accommodations? tickets for college events?)

I really wasn't looking forward to attending orientation in July. It turned out to be the best thing that could have happened. I met some other poli sci majors and we signed up for the same section for our American Government and Politics class. I bought some of my textbooks and opened up a bank account. I feel that I can relax a little bit more the rest of the summer now that I have made a few connections already.

S<small>TUDENT</small> R<small>EFLECTION</small>

Since orientation began just before move-in day, we were grateful for all the information we received from the college during the summer months. Our experience at orientation gave us the opportunity to meet some key people and ask the right questions.

P<small>ARENT</small> R<small>EFLECTION</small>

I must admit that my husband and I weren't too excited about attending orientation. Although it was a different school, this was our second child attending college, and we thought we knew it all. We were pleasantly surprised that our participation turned out to be very positive. Having already gone through this experience, we knew what kinds of questions to ask, and we were able to share our stories with other parents who were sending a child to college for the first time.

P<small>ARENT</small> R<small>EFLECTION</small>

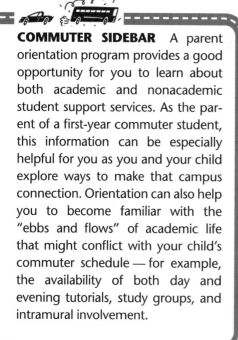

COMMUTER SIDEBAR A parent orientation program provides a good opportunity for you to learn about both academic and nonacademic student support services. As the parent of a first-year commuter student, this information can be especially helpful for you as you and your child explore ways to make that campus connection. Orientation can also help you to become familiar with the "ebbs and flows" of academic life that might conflict with your child's commuter schedule — for example, the availability of both day and evening tutorials, study groups, and intramural involvement.

Orientation Checklist

☑ Be prepared not to see your child very much at orientation. Many orientation programs are designed to provide separate experiences for parent and student.

☑ Be flexible. Take cues from your child. Don't be surprised if he or she decides to spend more time with peers.

☑ Arrive with an open mind; there is always something new to learn.

☑ Connect with as many parents as you can. Sharing experiences with each other is an important part of the program.

☑ Take notes. Information may not seem important right now, but as the year progresses, it will be.

☑ Don't be afraid to ask questions.

☑ If orientation takes place in the summer, start a "what-to-bring-in-September list": room furnishings, planners, a computer, and so forth.

☑ Check out miscellaneous items: banking, laundry facilities, transportation, safety, shopping, meal plans, computer services, and so on.

☑ Check important dates. Consider travel reservations and plans for family weekend.

Ready or Not

June, July, and August

> 🐦 *My son came back from orientation filled with excitement. He couldn't wait to get back to school and settle in. He experienced sadness as he said good-bye to friends, but tried to stay busy packing, working, and shopping for school supplies. I don't think he was ever afraid or scared, maybe just a bit apprehensive about how college would be different from high school.*
>
> PARENT OF A FIRST-YEAR COLLEGE STUDENT

The summer months before college begins for your child can be a real mixed bag of activities and emotions. They can be a busy time of preparing, packing, and shopping. You might feel great excitement and anxious anticipation, or you might sit back and reflect thoughtfully on all your child has accomplished and on the times yet to come. As the summer progresses, be aware of the many emotional ups and downs that you and your child may face.

June, July, and August can also be a time to communicate some of your own concerns and expectations. Focusing on issues such as money, personal safety, alcohol, and drugs can set an important tone as your child prepares for this new college experience.

SUMMER ISSUES

The Student

1. I'm excited and a little anxious about meeting new friends.

2. I want to communicate my feelings, but sometimes it's hard.

3. I want to separate from my parents, but I still need their reassurance.

4. I have great expectations!

5. I'm worried about course registration.

6. I hate good-byes.

7. I'm excited about college, but I have some doubts.

8. Packing and moving out is such a new thing.

9. What will it be like to live at home and commute?

10. How will I keep long-distance friendships alive?

11. Sometimes I have second thoughts about going to college.

12. I often question my decision-making skills.

13. I wonder what my dorm room will be like?

14. What if I don't like my roommate?

The Parent

1. Letting go is really difficult.

2. I want to communicate my feelings, but sometimes it's hard.

3. I'm anxious to get some answers to all my questions.

4. I should check out health insurance for my college-bound student.

5. Are my expectations for my child reasonable?

6. I hate good-byes.

7. I'm full of anticipation.

8. Helping my child pack up and move is fun, but it's also sad.

9. How will I adjust to my child living at home and commuting to college?

Emotional Ups and Downs

> 🐾 *The summer prior to our son's leaving for school, we had the,
> "Well, I'm going to college soon, so I don't have to pay attention to
> your rules anymore" discussion. I had been warned by friends of
> mine that the talk would be imminent, and I found that it did
> indeed pop its head quite early into the summer. That is when your
> child becomes a college freshman in spirit and action, before he
> ever leaves home. Somehow in his mind he had graduated from
> high school and entered college all in about twenty-four hours.*
>
> PARENT REFLECTION

During the summer months, students may experience a whole range of
emotions as they prepare to leave for college. Some may still be dealing
with feelings of loss associated with their high school graduation. Others
may feel anxious about the new experience that awaits them. Whatever
your student is feeling, this emotional shifting of gears can be unsettling.

The last few months of high school were probably filled with many activities and traditions for your child. Whether it was a memorable prom or
a stately graduation ceremony, all of these events represent significant mile-
stones for your student. It is important for you to understand the emotional
roller-coaster your child may be experiencing. On the one hand, he or she
may be experiencing the highs: excitement, exhilaration, anticipation, and
great expectations. On the other hand, your student may be perplexed by
the periods of significant lows: feelings of loss, anxiety, and self-doubt.

For most students, high school graduation is a symbolic rite of passage.
When the celebrations and parties come to an end, summer begins, but it is
no longer the lazy, hazy days of summer. Your child is entering a summer
unlike any other. Connections with friends, familiar support systems, and a
comfortable living environment are all about to change dramatically. As
you might expect, these changes will also affect life at home for you and
your child.

Your child may manifest ambivalence in a variety of ways. He or she
may begin to question recent decisions. *Did I choose the right college for the
right reasons? Should I have gone to the same college as my best friend? Did I declare the right major? Can I meet the academic challenges of my new school?*

Thoughts and feelings about relationships take hold too. *Will my best
friend always be there for me? How can I keep my connections with my family and
still be independent? How easily will I be able to make new friends? Will my
roommate like me?*

> ❧ *As time grew closer for our son to leave, he seemed much more apprehensive. He kept wondering if he had chosen the right college. He also commented more than once that he should have done better on his SATs and was already talking about transferring to another school after one semester. This created pangs of anxiety for all of us. We tried to validate his choice and let him know that a lot of his friends were probably feeling the same way he was.*
>
> PARENT REFLECTION

Your student may react in other ways as well. You may notice your child spending more time at home with family or spending every moment with friends before they go their separate ways. Your child also may change the way he or she deals with responsibility — taking on more, doing less. Emotionally, your son or daughter may manifest feelings by being impatient, overly critical, or needy. What makes things worse is that college-students-to-be often do not realize why they are feeling the way they are.

> ❧ *The last few weeks were stressful as friends went off one by one, trying to prepare for the big separation while attending to day-to-day responsibilities. Patience runs short, but parents need to realize the roller-coaster of emotions and not take the sarcasm personally.*
>
> PARENT REFLECTION

Changes in your child's emotions can affect you as well. As you are trying to understand the reactions of your student, you are attempting to cope with your own set of emotions associated with your child's departure. It can be a difficult balance.

During this time of transition, you need to be mindful of verbal and nonverbal messages you may send to your son or daughter. Here are some strategies to help you communicate with your child during these summer months.

Strategies for Parents

➤ Let your child know that **it is natural to have doubts**.

➤ Encourage your student to respond in his or her own way; there is **no one correct way to deal with leaving home**.

➤ Make sure your student knows that **change is exciting**, but it can also be stressful.

➠ **Show confidence in your child's choices**. If you have doubts, your son or daughter will too.

➠ **Focus on your child's strengths**. Successes in high school are what got him or her to this point.

➠ Plan a time when you and your student can **sort through incoming information** and take appropriate action (for example, complete forms, pay deposits).

➠ Don't look for a quick fix to changing emotions. There isn't one. **Listen empathetically**, and reassure your child that these feelings are normal.

➠ **Don't overreact to mood changes**. Your child's sensitivity and irritability may not have a direct cause, and so your child may not be able to explain it.

➠ Let your child know by what you say and do that **his or her role in the family has not changed**. Although your child is leaving, he or she is not being abandoned.

➠ If you are a **single-parent household**, realize that your child may have more difficulty leaving one parent, and you may experience feelings of being left behind.

➠ Be aware of your own **emotional ups and downs**.

Living on Campus

Living in a residence hall and adjusting to roommates can present some major challenges for first-year students. Overall, a roommate experience can have a powerful impact on a student's overall adjustment.

Residence hall structures vary from institution to institution. In most traditional halls, options include singles, doubles, triples, and quads. Some colleges offer suites that have single or double rooms off a common living area. Apartments or townhouses may be available for upperclass students. Colleges offer many housing options: single-sex halls, coeducational halls, special-interest or theme-related housing such as honors, substance-free halls, or first-year-experience halls. In most cases, large state-operated institutions have more housing options. At many smaller, private institutions, first-year students and sophomores may be required to live on campus, but housing for upperclass students is often at a premium. More and more of these schools cannot guarantee four years of on-campus housing. Many schools have an off-campus housing office to assist juniors and seniors in locating suitable apartments in the surrounding communities.

You and your student need to be aware of the housing options and policies for your chosen college. You will benefit from taking the time to familiarize yourselves with all the options and policies. Pay close attention to residential choices, the roommate assignment process, and room change policies and procedures. This information is usually found in the student handbook, at the office of residence life, through specific mailings, or in a separate residential handbook. Take the time to discuss with your son or daughter what concerns you may have about housing issues. However, remember that it is your student who must ultimately make housing decisions and take the responsibility for his or her living situation.

A college usually makes housing decisions with the help of information provided by a housing questionnaire. The questionnaire provides an opportunity for your child to share information that can help the college find a compatible roommate. The questions are usually about personal habits such as waking and sleeping hours, study habits, and special interests. It is important that your student be totally honest on the questionnaire. That it is the first step toward a smooth transition to campus living. Sometimes students misrepresent themselves on the questionnaire because they are afraid their parents will find out something they have kept hidden from them. This is often the case for students who smoke. There can be disastrous results if a smoker and a nonsmoker are assigned as roommates. Most colleges have non-smoking halls or floors.

The housing questionnaire will also ask your student to indicate housing preferences. In most cases, he or she will be asked to list first, second, and third choices for a specific residence hall structure or type of room. Remember that there is no ideal situation. Much depends on the individual's personal habits, unique personality, ability to live with others, and need for privacy. Some students report that a single room can be isolating for a first-year student, and a triple can create more problems than a quad because of the odd number of students living together. For example, two roommates may find they have a lot in common and spend considerable time together. As a result, the third roommate may feel left out.

If theme halls are available, your child should consider the pros and cons of such an arrangement. The idea of living together with students who have a particular interest or major in common can be attractive to a student who is looking to bond with peers early on. Students with similar interests often share the same kind of personal study habits, which may be more conducive to a harmonious living situation. On the other hand, some students may feel too isolated living only with students who share their same interests or major.

First-year-experience programs sometimes provide another housing option. These programs usually provide a weekly or biweekly evening seminar focusing on a specific first-year adjustment issue such as campus involvement, wellness, or academic challenges. Some students may welcome the opportunity to live with and attend some classes with a group of students in a first-year-experience program; others may feel this experience to be too limiting. Students have different needs, and colleges try to provide as many choices as possible to accommodate these needs.

While your son or daughter needs to decide what housing situation might be the best personal fit, deciding between a single-sex hall or a coeducational hall may be more complex. If you as a parent have strong views about this issue, you need to discuss them openly and honestly with your child. This is a good time to talk about your family values and expectations and provide an opportunity for a frank and open discussion. You and your child should think through the pros and cons of single-sex versus coeducational halls. Some people feel that a coeducational hall provides an extra measure of security. However, a student who has strong feelings about privacy might be more comfortable in a single-sex hall. Obviously, a student living in a coed hall must be comfortable and behave appropriately with members of the opposite sex.

Roommates

> *I did room freshman year with someone I knew from before. I think it helped me a lot because she was someone I could go out with to other functions and meet other people. We ended up having very different friends during college, but she and I have remained friends ever since. I think it is important to have realistic expectations. I know a few people who lived with best friends from high school, and it was a disaster.*
>
> STUDENT REFLECTION

When assigning roommates, most colleges take into account the information that students provide on the housing questionnaire. Factors that affect compatibility include study habits, sleeping habits, and personal habits. In many instances, although a choice cannot be guaranteed, your student may be asked for the name of a particular person or persons that he or she would like to room with.

Students who indicate a particular roommate preference should consider the pros and cons of that choice. For example, your child may decide to room with a friend from high school. This arrangement certainly brings about an initial sense of security. They know one another and therefore do not have to deal with those first awkward, ice-breaking moments. On the other hand, old friends who live together may have some unrealistic expectations that can cause problems. There is often a sense that their friendship will remain the same and that things will continue on as they did in high school. In reality, however, relationships can become quite different during the college years.

As these students become accustomed to their new college environment, they begin to branch out into new areas. They may take different classes and join different campus organizations. Soon they may go in different directions and meet new people. Considerable tension can arise when they feel betrayed by their old friend. Some students begin to feel smothered by their high school friend, and some become upset that the relationship has changed. Others are surprised by some of their friend's personal habits that they were not aware of.

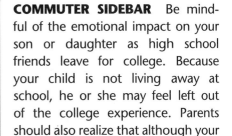

COMMUTER SIDEBAR Be mindful of the emotional impact on your son or daughter as high school friends leave for college. Because your child is not living away at school, he or she may feel left out of the college experience. Parents should also realize that although your college student is living at home, there will be new time demands. Remember to review your expectations and readjust household responsibilities and curfews.

Sometimes students who meet for the first time at summer orientation will request to live together. Again, the security of knowing someone, even briefly, can be an attractive alternative to being assigned to live with someone the student has never met before. However, making a decision about someone based on a brief positive encounter can sometimes set up unrealistic expectations in a living situation. If your student chooses a roommate rather than being assigned one by the college, he or she should realize that there are no guarantees that the situation will work out for the better.

Sometime during the summer, your student will receive notification of his or her roommate for the coming year. Many questions will probably race through your child's head. *Will my roommate like me? How compatible will we be? Will we get along?* Once again, communication is the key. Encourage your child to talk openly with his or her roommate and make joint decisions about their living space, the television, the refrigerator, the CD players, and so on.

> Our son chose to commute so that he could continue working. Our concern was that in doing so, he would not fully know the "college experience." We want him to enjoy college, build lasting relationships, and feel a part of his school. I must confess, however, that I was a bit

relieved when he decided to commute. As a mother, I was not looking forward to seeing him only during holidays and vacations.

PARENT REFLECTION

Communicating Expectations

> *We had our son doing his own laundry about sophomore year in high school. Not only did it help him learn to be prepared for college (at that time, a far off motivation), but it actually helped cut down on the laundry! What I had discovered was that his perfectly acceptable way of cleaning his room (which was periodically required by me) was to take everything that was on the floor, on the chair, bed, and anywhere else and put it all in the laundry. Once he began to do his own, his cleaning skills also improved!*

PARENT REFLECTION

As a parent, communicating your expectations at this time can be a delicate process. You want to reinforce your child's autonomy, but you also want to communicate your expectations and values. Expectations exist on different levels. Some expectations relate to personal values that can affect how your child deals with relationships, peer pressure, alcohol use or abuse, and so on. Other types of expectations focus on coping and life skills — practical issues such as managing a budget, doing laundry, and nutritional concerns.

At some point during the summer, it is important to determine when and how you are going to approach these issues with your child. If orientation occurs early in the summer, it can serve as a springboard for discussion. Obviously each family has its own style of communication, but how you communicate your expectations at this transitional time can set the tone for your future relationship with your child. Notice how your child communicates best with you, with authority figures, and with peers. Think about discussions you have had together in the past. Then reflect on what has been effective. There is a good chance that what worked before will work now. This is not the time to change how you and your child communicate.

Reflecting on the following questions will help you to determine how to communicate with your soon-to-be college student and what you may need to discuss:

▶ How aware is my child of his or her strengths and weaknesses?

▶ How does my child approach new experiences?

▶ Is my child comfortable asking questions? Taking risks? Meeting new people?

▶ Is my child a self-starter?

▶ Does my child tend to procrastinate? Become easily overwhelmed?

▶ How well will my child be able to handle new freedoms?

The parental strategies we offer here will make it easier for you to communicate your expectations with your child.

Strategies for Parents

➼ Ask open-ended questions. Remember that the goal is to **keep communication open**, not to close it. Try not to sound as if you are preaching. When you are trying to get your point across, use the word *I* rather than *you*: *"I know you're aware that peer pressure can be tough to deal with."* vs. *"You better work hard to be a leader rather than just following the crowd."*

➼ **Be open and honest about your values and expectations** on sensitive subjects such as alcohol, drugs, and sex. State your views without coming across as judgmental.

➼ Remember that **listening is part of communicating**. Being a good sounding board is an important part of the process.

➼ **Expect to disagree** on some issues. Keep in mind that your student is struggling for independence and autonomy.

➼ Take some extra time to **communicate your support and encouragement**. Positive feedback is especially important for your child at this time.

Money Issues

> 🐚 *Senior year in high school, we opened a joint checking account for our son. Into that he deposited his work monies, gifts, or monies from his dad and me. He then had to write checks and balance the account. He used this same account initially when he started school, but then decided to open another in the town in which his college was located. He felt well prepared to deal with that issue.*
>
> PARENT REFLECTION

Before your student leaves for school, take some time to discuss money matters. Your definition of money management may be very different from your child's. Be sure to cover issues such as credit cards, banking needs, and spending money beyond books and tuition.

Some money decisions depend on the banking facilities and resources available at your child's college. Many colleges provide full banking services for students. Others have more limited services that might include ATM machines, check cashing, or banks within walking distance. In order to avoid money problems, be sure you are well informed about the banking services available for your student.

Your conversations about money should include discussions about how to handle expenses beyond tuition, room, and board. Some parents make it clear from the very beginning that their child is responsible for his or her own spending money (for things such as snacks, magazines, and movies) and for purchasing personal items (toiletries such as shampoo, toothpaste, and deodorant). Consider the following items when putting together your student's budget:

- Textbooks

- Telephone bill

- Personal items (e.g., toothpaste, shampoo)

- Clothing

- Laundry

- Entertainment and snacks

- Transportation (holiday and weekend travel, car expenses for students who have a car)

- Miscellaneous spending money

In many cases, students save up enough money from a summer job to cover personal expenses. Some parents provide their child with a lump sum of spending money each semester. Others provide a monthly allotment. Many colleges offer debit card systems that allow parents to deposit monies into an account their student can charge against.

One important thing your child should learn is how much money it takes to live. For the most part, students tend to be unaware of the cost of personal items since parents have usually purchased them. Most students bring items such as toothpaste and detergent with them when they first come to college. It is not until they have to replace these items for themselves that they begin to realize the cost of living.

Although putting a large sum of money into your student's account may seem like the easiest solution, it is not a good idea unless your child has had an opportunity to acquire reasonable money management skills. The tendency to spend too much and too soon can have a negative impact on your child's personal and academic life. For example, students who spend all their money quickly sometimes decide to get a job without their parents' knowledge. Their grades may suffer as a result.

Remember to discuss the use of a credit card with your student before school begins and from time to time throughout the academic year. Many credit card companies visit college campuses, offering attractive packages to entice students to sign up. Your student can easily acquire a credit card without your knowledge or signature. If you feel that your child will need a credit card, apply for one before school starts. Then you can co-sign an agreement with your child, which allows for a low limit on charges. If it is important for your student to have a card for emergencies, then be sure that "emergencies" are well defined. As one college accounting faculty member advises, "Try to make some time to discuss with your child how he or she will budget for spending needs and address unexpected costs. Be aware that students may use credit cards to finance additional personal expenditures that can quickly lead to overspending."

Here are some ideas for handling those tough money issues.

Strategies for Parents

▸▸ Start talking in the summer about costs. Provide your student with an **estimated price list of personal items**. Better yet, take your child shopping for items he or she may need regularly, such as shampoo and soap.

▸▸ Be aware of the college's policy for use of a **debit card**. Some colleges allow students to charge everything from bookstore items to campus movies, while others are more limiting.

▸▸ Know how the college handles **telephone bills** (limits for bills, ID numbers, and so forth). Before telephone bills add up, decide how they will be paid. Calling cards can be an expensive convenience, so set limits early.

▸▸ **Be clear about your expectations**. Students need to be aware that if they push the limit, there will be consequences.

▸▸ Agree to **revisit the subject of money from time to time**. If you keeping the lines of communication open, you will give your child the message that it is okay to make mistakes. Encourage your son or daughter to be honest and forthcoming about problems in order to avoid excessive bills, overdue charges, and the like.

Will My Child Be Safe?

> *We've had more than one conversation this summer about making good decisions concerning personal safety. I know that my daughter is a responsible young woman, but she sometimes can be too trusting. Talking about these issues has been a real challenge. I want my daughter to feel comfortable in her new surroundings, but I also want her to be aware of the precautions she needs to take, especially when she is out at night.*
>
> PARENT REFLECTION

Campus safety and security issues are of major concern to most parents today. These issues were highlighted with the 1990 passage of the Students' Right to Know and Campus Security Act, which requires all institutions that receive federal funds to publicize yearly crime statistics. The 1998 Clery Act mandates that colleges provide and publish written descriptions of all safety and security policies, procedures, and programs.

No college can be considered crime free. Colleges do have the responsibility, however, to set up systems and procedures designed to address personal and property safety. They must make available appropriate resources and support services for students who may be victims of crime. They also must provide opportunities for students to learn how to take responsibility for their personal safety.

Although responsibilities may vary, most colleges have their own security department that oversees the safety and welfare of the college community. At some schools, security officials have the power to arrest, while at other institutions, campus security may do the initial reporting and then refer incidents to the local or state police. In any case, many colleges are working in the best interest of the students to develop a healthy relationship between campus officials and local law enforcement agencies.

In order to maintain a safe and secure environment, most campuses have a number of systems in place. At many colleges, emergency telephones are placed strategically throughout the campus and monitored by campus security or police twenty-four hours a day. Some telephones, when accessed, flash a light that indicates an urgent need for assistance. An escort service is another common security measure on college campuses. This service is particularly helpful for students who may need to walk alone in the evening. Many colleges also provide shuttle services on campus and the surrounding area. Information on how and where to access shuttle or escort services is usually posted throughout the campus on bulletin boards, in campus newspapers, on the college's web site, and in residence halls.

The protection and security of students living in campus housing facilities is a major priority for colleges. Many halls control access through an electric card system. Some schools also have desk monitors present at certain hours who are usually students serving as "paraprofessional" security guards. These students may be paid, but sometimes they serve in a volunteer capacity.

Although colleges may have numerous security systems in place, students sometimes do not take advantage of them. Many students think that they are invincible. Moreover, they view their new environment as a safe haven where no harm can come to them. As a result, they sometimes make unwise or careless decisions — not locking dorm rooms, propping building doors open, walking alone at night in poorly lit areas — that put themselves and other members of the college community at risk. Early in the year, students need to understand the role they play in taking responsibility for their own safety.

To help in this process, many colleges provide educational programs designed to inform and educate students about issues related to safety and security. At orientation for new students, students and parents are flooded with information about security measures, reporting procedures, and support services. During the course of the year, the college may provide residence floor meetings, special speakers, and informal discussions to get important messages across to students concerning these issues. Some colleges even sponsor a "Safety and Security Week" involving campus security and local law enforcement officials. All of these programs try to convey how important it is for the college and the student to work together to ensure a safe and healthy environment.

Sexual Assault The reality of campus life brings with it significant challenges for students in regard to their own personal safety. This is particularly true for first-year students whose need to fit in and make new friends may be accompanied by a too-trusting view of their new environment. Additional involvement with alcohol or drugs may further compromise a student's ability to make responsible judgments. All of these factors contribute to college students' being more vulnerable to incidents of sexual assault than any other specific population.

Most colleges take a proactive approach in addressing the issues of sexual harassment, sexual assault, and date rape or acquaintance rape. In accordance with federal guidelines, colleges must publish written policies that usually include a definition of terms, behavioral standards, and discipline sanctions for offenders. The guidelines also explain the procedures for filing a complaint with campus officials, as well as with the local police. Information about on-campus and community support systems such as medical facilities, emergency hot-line telephone numbers, and crisis and counseling centers is also included in those guidelines.

Many colleges spend a significant amount of time and effort presenting educational programs during the academic year that are designed to educate students on the issue of sexual assault. Such programs usually include some discussion about the role of alcohol and drugs in regard to this issue. Loss of control, impairment of judgment, and the lowering of defenses are some of the effects of alcohol and drugs that contribute to students' vulnerability and may put them at considerable risk. Some colleges provide information about date rape drugs that can easily be slipped into an individual's unattended drink. Within a short period of time, these drugs can cause drowsiness, confusion, or amnesia. If they are mixed with alcohol, the results can be lethal.

Parents should consider taking some time before classes begin to discuss safety and security issues with their child. Some of the strategies listed below can help you generate a healthy dialogue that will communicate your support as well as your expectations.

Strategies for Parents

➦ Review with your child the **campus security measures** outlined in the student handbook and other college publications. Make sure your student is aware of campus crime statistics so he or she will get the message that no one is immune to crime.

➦ Encourage your student to take advantage of **shuttles, escort systems, and other security services**. Urge your child to be aware of the surroundings and the neighborhood areas around the college. Remind him or her always to walk in well-lit areas and to avoid walking or jogging alone at night.

➦ Express your concerns about **date rape or acquaintance rape**. Tell your daughter to be assertive and avoid giving mixed messages. Tell your son not to make unwarranted assumptions and to accept that "no" means "no."

➦ Discuss the connections between **alcohol, drugs, and sexual assault**. Emphasize that in order to make good judgments, a person needs to be in control. If your child goes to a party with friends, encourage him or her to leave with those same friends. Suggest that transportation arrangements be planned in advance.

▶▶ Stress to your student the need to be knowledgeable about **campus resources and reporting procedures**. Encourage him or her to keep emergency telephone numbers for medical assistance and counseling services close at hand.

Alcohol Issues The issue of alcohol use and abuse by college students continues to be a nationwide problem. Campuses continue to look for new and creative ways to address college student drinking. "College Parents of America" has taken a leadership role in working towards providing parents with assistance about how they can play a part in addressing this issue. The following recommendations may be of help to you as you discuss your own expectations with your child.

College Parents of America Outlines Eight Points for Parents Speaking with Their Students About Alcohol

Any parent who reads the newspaper or watches news on television has seen and heard tragic stories about the excessive drinking on campus. Parents are frightened by these stories and have every right to be.

As a resource, advisor and advocate for the more than 32 million households with parents of current and future college students throughout the United States, College Parents of America (CPA) shares this concern. CPA is advising parents to talk with their children about the impact of binge drinking on their lives and their responsibilities to themselves and to their peers. CPA also is negotiating for possible insurance incentives for students signing pledges against binge drinking and drinking and driving. In addition, CPA is working to further involve parents and other parties in individual campus and other local efforts to combat alcohol abuse on campus. In cooperation with William DeJong, Director of the Higher Education Center, and Linda Devine, Assistant Dean of Student Life at the University of Oregon, College Parents of America is encouraging parents to regularly speak with their students about alcohol and offers the following eight talking points.

1. **Set clear and realistic expectations regarding academic performance**.

   Studies conducted nationally have demonstrated that partying may contribute as much to a student's decline in grades as the difficulty of his or her academic work. If students know their parents expect sound academic work, they are likely to be more devoted to their studies and have less time to get in trouble with alcohol.

Speaking with Your Child About Alcohol

2. **Stress to your student that alcohol is toxic and excessive consumption can fatally poison.**
   This is not a scare tactic. The fact is students die every year from alcohol poisoning. Discourage dangerous drinking through participation in drinking games, fraternity hazing or in any other way. Parents should ask their students to also have the courage to intervene when they see someone putting their life at risk through participation in dangerous drinking.

3. **Tell students to intervene when classmates are in trouble with alcohol.**
   Nothing is more tragic than an unconscious student being left to die while others either fail to recognize that the student is in jeopardy or fail to call for help due to fear of getting the student in trouble.

4. **Tell students to stand up for their right to a safe academic environment.**
   Students who do not drink can be affected by the behavior of those who do, ranging from interrupted study time to assault or unwanted sexual advances. Students can confront these problems directly by discussing them with the offender. If that fails, they should notify the housing director or other residence hall staff.

5. **Know about the alcohol scene on campus and talk to students about it.**
   Students grossly exaggerate the use of alcohol and other drugs by their peers. A recent survey found that University of Oregon students believed 96 percent of their peers drink alcohol at least once a week, when the actual rate was 52 percent. Students are highly influenced by peers and tend to drink up to what they perceive to be the norm. Confronting misperceptions about alcohol use is vital.

6. **Avoid tales of drinking exploits from your own college years.**
   Entertaining students with stories of drinking back in "the good old days" normalizes what, even then, was abnormal behavior. It also appears to give parental approval to dangerous alcohol consumption.

7. **Encourage your student to volunteer in community work.**
   In addition to structuring free time, volunteerism provides students with opportunities to develop job-related skills and to gain valuable experience. Helping others also gives students a broader outlook and a healthier perspective on the opportunities they enjoy. Volunteer work on campus helps students further connect with their school, increasing the likelihood of staying in college.

8. **Make it clear — Underage alcohol consumption and driving after drinking are against the law.**

   Parents should make it clear that they do not condone breaking the law. Parents of college students should openly and clearly express disapproval of underage drinking and dangerous alcohol consumption. And, if parents themselves drink, they should present a positive role model in the responsible use of alcohol.

   Talk with your student about alcohol. While parents may not be able to actively monitor students away from home, they can be available to talk and listen, and that is just as important. It can do more than help shape lives — it can save lives.

Reprinted by permission of College Parents of America from, "College Parents of America Outline Eight Points for Parents Speaking with Their Students About Alcohol." College Parents of America (CPA) is a resource, advisor and advocate for the more than 32 million households with parents of current and future college students throughout the United States. CPA is the only national membership association dedicated to helping parents prepare and put their children through college easily, economically and safely. CPA provides new information on saving strategies, financial aid, education tax credits and deductions and other ways to help pay for college; offers valuable advice during the application and selection process; advises parents on the individual opportunities and challenges they will encounter during their students' college year; and serves as their advocate on Capitol Hill, in state capitals and on the nation's campuses. In addition, CPA offers families special values on products and services.

For more on College Parents of America, call toll-free 1-888-256-4627 for automated information and an application, locally at 202-661-2170, visit **www.collegeparents.org** on the Internet or write to College Parents of America, 700 Thirteenth Street, N.W., Suite 950, Washington, DC 20005.

What About Drugs? Although alcohol is the drug of choice for college students today, students' illicit use of substances other than alcohol continues to be a major area of concern for campuses around the country. Some students experiment with drugs for the first time when they enter college, while others have already started casual use while in high school or even earlier. Reasons for drug use might include peer pressure, curiosity, stress reduction, enhancement of sensations or performance, and social experimentation. No matter what the reason, drugs are dangerous and can sometimes lead to catastrophic results.

Drug use presents many serious physiological and emotional consequences. Some of these are depression, sleep deprivation, loss of memory, mood swings, irritability, intense highs and lows, hallucinations, hyperactivity, rapid pulse, and respiratory distress. Their use can affect all aspects of an individual's behavior. They can interfere with a student's ability to learn and can hinder academic performance.

Drugs

Substance abuse, nevertheless, is a reality of campus life. When addressing the issue of alcohol with your child, you need to convey clear messages and expectations. Part of this message should also include a discussion about drug use. Straightforward discussions should take place before your student begins college and should be revisited from time to time during his or her college career.

In order to be effective when addressing this issue, you should have some general knowledge about the campus drug scene. Myths need to be dispelled and replaced with accurate facts. Web sites, information hot lines, and bookstores all provide up-to-date information on drugs and their consequences.

Parents should be careful not to glamorize any experiences they may have had with drugs during their own college days. You need to dispel the idea that the use of drugs is just another rite of passage and make clear that drug use does not fit into any plan for success. Experimentation and casual use can lead to dependency and the use of other drugs. For example, the use of marijuana, which was in vogue more than a decade ago, has once again become a popular drug of choice among young people. It is considered a "gateway drug," one that often leads to more progressive drug use and the adoption of a drug-using lifestyle.

When discussing your concerns, be sure that your child is aware of "club drugs" — Ecstasy, Ketamine (CAT), Rohypnol (Roofies), methamphetamine (Ice, Speed, Fire) and LSD — drugs that are colorless and odorless and cannot be detected in beverages. These drugs can cause major health problems and can be even more dangerous when they are mixed with alcohol. Leaving drinks unattended at parties or bars, drinking from another person's glass, or taking beverages from punch bowls or pitchers are dangerous practices.

In compliance with federal guidelines, colleges have implemented programs and policies designed to prevent the illicit use of drugs and the abuse of alcohol. Students should know that if they violate these polices, they will face college discipline sanctions. In most cases, they will also be referred to local law enforcement officials, who will impose legal sanctions as well. According to federal law, these students also place themselves in jeopardy of losing any financial aid provided through federal funding.

Broaching this subject with your student before he or she leaves for college is a good starting point. Asking questions during the year about friends, activities, and spending habits in a forthright and genuinely caring manner can help you get a sense of your child's bigger picture. Don't be afraid to share your concerns. Remember, the excuse that "everyone is doing it" needs to be challenged. Addressing these issues is a challenge that every parent must meet.

Leaving for College

> ❧ *I must admit that as the time drew closer for my daughter to leave for college, I felt more and more anxious. As I drove away and left her at the dorm, I began to realize that a brand-new relationship with my daughter had begun. I was excited for her, but sad that I could no longer think of her as my little girl.*
>
> PARENT REFLECTION

As the summer months come to a close, your child is saying good-bye to friends, finishing up a summer job, and focusing on getting ready to leave for college. Your mind is probably full of emotions that are still running high, and it is time for you to take care of some practical matters: *What needs to be done? What has my student forgotten to pack? Whom do I still need to contact?*

Packing for college can be a symbolic, memorable experience. It can be an emotional outlet for your child as he or she copes with move-in-day anxieties. Students typically underpack and then overpack. They change from one activity to another, first moving slowly and then rushing at breakneck speed. Sometimes disorganized, sometimes planful, your student goes about getting ready to leave.

For you as a parent, it is important that you do not overreact to all these changes. Make suggestions about what to bring, but respect your child's right to make decisions. What may seem important to you may not be a priority for your son or daughter. Take cues from your child. Communicate your concerns without sounding preachy or judgmental.

> ❧ *Our son approached packing as if he was leaving home forever, never to return again. Everything he owned appeared to be going with him. Reminding him that we would be visiting at school in October only seemed to be more unsettling for him. At that point, we felt the best way to go would be to just let him make his own decisions about what to pack.*
>
> PARENT REFLECTION

As move-in day arrives, saying good-bye takes on many dimensions. Tearful encounters, final hugs (for the family pets too), and last-minute conversations with family and friends dominate this time. As your grown-up child says good-bye to familiar surroundings in his or her own

Packing for College

Moving in

unique way, feelings of loss and separation may overwhelm you and your child.

> ৰ্ঠৈ *It was very difficult to let go — truly traumatic to say good-bye as our son said good-bye to his siblings. The sadness was consuming, but at the same time we were excited about his future. All of these mixed feelings left us feeling very drained.*
>
> PARENT REFLECTION

For some students, the final good-bye may happen before boarding a plane, a train, or a bus to travel to a new environment. For others, it may involve packing up the family car and getting ready for the drive to campus. In every case, it can be an emotionally draining experience for everyone.

Once on campus, your student may encounter what appears to be chaos. Simple tasks such as finding a parking place close to his or her new residence may prove to be frustrating. Your student may wait in long lines to check in and spend time unpacking, arranging room furnishings, meeting roommates, and finding his or her way around new territory. These things can be both exciting and unsettling.

More than likely, you and your child will experience a full range of emotions. If there is a lot of tension in the air, you may have a difficult time anticipating what your child is feeling at the moment. It is important for you to stay calm and not get impatient. Remember that you want to say good-bye to your student on a positive note. There is no easy way to prepare for this process of letting go as you leave for the trip home.

> ৰ্ঠৈ *After everyone moved in, the college our daughter attends had a big barbecue for all freshmen and their parents. We were glad that we had this excuse to spend a little bit more time with her before we had to leave. Funny, though, as we watched her connect with some students she had met at summer orientation, reality began to set in. We knew things would be different from now on. When she came up to us and asked for a bit more spending money, we almost felt relieved to hear this familiar request once again. Needless to say, it was a bumpy ride home for a lot of reasons.*
>
> PARENT REFLECTION

Monthly Checklist: Getting Ready to Leave

 Refer to your "what-to-bring-in-September list" as move-in day approaches.

☑ Plan ahead. Be aware of move-in dates and times designated by the residence life office.

☑ Be sure that insurance coverage is addressed before classes begin.

☑ Decide on a meal plan.

☑ Make sure that all forms (health, financial aid, residential life) have been submitted.

☑ Decide on how money matters will be handled (banking, checking account, etc.).

☑ Be clear about and plan for computer needs and campus systems.

☑ Agree on how you plan to keep in touch (e.g., calling card, e-mail).

☑ Check on the availability of transportation systems.

Reality Sets In
September

September

🙿 *I expected my daughter to have some concerns about adjusting to living away from home. Because she was such a good student in high school, I was caught off guard when she called to say she was overwhelmed with her courses. As a parent, how can I support her in adjusting to these new academic challenges?*

PARENT OF A FIRST-YEAR COLLEGE STUDENT

As the first semester of college begins, your student will probably be immersed in a flurry of activities. Finding the way around campus, attending classes, getting to know roommates, and becoming familiar with new faces are typical issues for new students. Adjusting to new academic demands and learning to manage time, as well as new-found freedoms, will present some significant challenges to your new college student.

Emotions at this time can range from excitement to anxiety and fear. You may experience some of those same feelings as you empathize with your child and respond to this new college adventure. Just as your child is learning to adjust to a brand-new environment, you will need to reconsider your role as you journey along this venture.

🙿 *I shared in my daughter's excitement and, of course, pointed out that she will have new freedoms and choices to make and that they would be her choices. My daughter is a responsible young woman thus far, but new freedoms can cloud even the best of people, so in typical mother-daughter fashion, I reminded her of the things and worries that will always be on my mind even though I am not there.*

PARENT REFLECTION

SEPTEMBER ISSUES

Student Issues

1. I'm really homesick.

2. Sometimes I'm really afraid to take risks.

3. I'm learning about self-discovery, but sometimes I'm not sure who I really am.

4. I've been lost too many times on campus. It was hard finding all my classes. At first, I had no idea where my mailbox was.

5. This is different from living at home. There I had lots of friends and family to talk to.

6. I really miss my friends from high school. I even miss my sister! Last Friday night I actually stayed in my dorm room and did nothing!

7. Sometimes my roommate is okay, but she sure gets up early. We ordered pizza in the other night — it was fun.

8. I thought I would make more friends by now.

9. I e-mailed my best friend from high school a week ago, and I still haven't heard back from her. I wonder if our friendship is going to last.

10. I never thought my classes would take up so much time. It's not working to do assignments the night before they are due.

11. My first test is coming up in a week. I'm afraid I'll fail it because I'm not keeping up with the work. I failed one quiz in that class already. I don't know when I'll get to the research paper.

12. I want to go to a party with my roommate this weekend, but I don't know if I have time. I've got a lot of homework.

13. The kids here really drink a lot at parties! I wonder how I'll fit in if I don't join in?

14. Sometimes it's hard to remember when my classes are. I completely missed a class last week because I didn't have it on my planner.

15. I'm not sure I like any of my classes. None of them has anything to do with my major.

16. I was really upset by what one of my professors said last week. It goes against everything I've ever been taught and against what I believe is right.

17. I'm sure going through money fast. I never realized it took so much money just to live!

18. At first, I really liked the food here. I think I liked it too much because I've gained ten pounds!

Parent Issues

1. It's really quiet and lonely at home without my child around.

2. The whole dynamics of our family has changed. The other children are different without their sibling around.

3. College expenses are more than I anticipated. Where is the money going to come from?

4. Sometimes my college student seems so grown up, adjusting well to college life. Then there are times when that same child really wants to give it all up and come home.

5. When my child is so unsure of the new environment, I don't know what to say.

6. My child seems more standoffish lately. We don't talk like we used to. How do I handle the increased impatience and short temper at times?

7. The other day, I got an e-mail from my maturing college student. He said how proud he was of us — his parents — for raising him so well and giving him such a happy childhood. Tears just flowed down my face.

• •

Homesickness

> *It was pretty hard being at the end of the telephone line with a tearful, anxious child. I had to hold myself back from saying, "Look, I'll come get you right now."*
>
> PARENT REFLECTION

Homesickness is a word that describes a whole range of feelings associated with a student's separation from his or her home base. Although school officials and parents commonly use this word, most students are reluctant to

Homesickness

use it to describe themselves. For many, the word implies a low level of maturity and a lack of independence. Therefore, parents should be careful not to use this word when responding to their child's feelings.

Remember that each student's experience is unique. Feelings of anxiety and apprehension are a natural part of the adjustment process. Some students get so caught up in the excitement of their new environment — meeting new people, attending first classes — that they gradually begin to feel at home. Others may feel so overwhelmed that it interferes with their ability to adjust.

Many students do admit that they miss talking with their siblings, taking their dog for a walk, or just hanging out with old friends. Mealtimes may trigger some momentary feelings of sadness for your child when the campus dining hall causes him or her to recall memories of the good food at home. The lack of privacy in the residence halls may cause your student to yearn for the comforts of his or her own space back home.

As a parent, be aware that college requires your child to adjust to new experiences — new friends, changed academics, a new living situation — as well as an adjustment to the losses of leaving behind old friends, siblings, and familiar surroundings. Some students may have more difficulty than others dealing with the losses. Their need to hold on to what has been safe and familiar may prevent them from actively engaging with their new environment. As a result, they may be reluctant to develop new relationships because they are afraid they will be betraying old high school friends. This may also affect their initial response to their roommates and their willingness to get involved in new activities and student organizations. Their inability to let go and move forward may cause some students to withdraw and become less motivated to assimilate into their new environment.

In the first few weeks of school, you may receive some very mixed messages from your student.

> *My daughter didn't express any concerns directly to me, but I overheard a conversation with her friends talking about her anxieties. "I am not afraid of the classes, but I'm afraid of college." I took that as the fear of the unknown. It seems to me that kids have an idea of what a college student is and have a hard time realizing they're there [a student at college]. It's much like when you first become a parent: you still feel like a son or a daughter, but now you're the parent!*
>
> PARENT REFLECTION

Many students do not like to admit that they are having difficulty with their transition from high school to college. They feel that admitting these feelings implies that they are not ready for college. Often people cope with their internal feelings of inadequacy by placing blame on their external world. Students may find fault with their professors, roommates, classes, food, or other things. It becomes easier to blame things they can't control rather than acknowledge their own feelings.

> Although my daughter said often she couldn't wait to move out and that she wouldn't get homesick, she was in fact homesick. She called almost twice each day. She had a difficult time setting up her computer, and she thought we'd probably drop everything and come help. But of course we couldn't.
>
> PARENT REFLECTION

Your student's reaction to homesickness will be varied. There may be frantic telephone calls, immediate pleas to come home, or overwhelming sadness and tearfulness. Your child might second-guess his or her college choice and express the desire to transfer after the first few weeks of the semester. How should you respond?

Strategies for Parents

➡ Don't overreact to those **first frantic telephone calls**. Listen carefully, and try to determine how best to address your child's need at that moment. Don't panic!

➡ Don't be surprised if your son or daughter expresses strong emotions one day, and then these feelings disappear the next day. It is not unusual to receive a call that "**nothing is going right**" or "I want to come home" — and then the next day, "**all is well**."

➡ Brainstorm options and a possible course of action with your student as problems arise. **Generating choices** with your child conveys that you care and also puts the responsibility on him or her for follow-up.

➡ Help your student **break down a larger problem** into smaller, more manageable issues. Identifying tasks that address each concern will help your child feel more in control of the situation.

➡ **Don't look for a quick fix**. There isn't one.

➡ To help with **homesickness** (and remember *not* to call it that), remind your student that residence life staff can be especially helpful. Encourage your child to seek out ways to become involved with student clubs and athletic programs in order to meet new people and feel more comfortable with the new environment.

➡ Encourage your child to seek out **campus support systems** for help with problems. Counseling and campus ministry can be especially helpful at this time.

➡ When it comes to telephone calls and visits home, it is important to be flexible. There is no hard rule of thumb. **Some students may need to connect more often than others**.

➡ Sometimes you may not know what to say, but just listening to your child's concerns can fill a much-needed void. It is important for you to **convey your encouragement and reassurance**.

➡ **A care package from home**, including food, notes and so forth, might be just the thing to brighten the mood.

Roommate Adjustments

> ✒ *My brother is in his first year at college, and his roommate goes home every weekend. He really feels alone. I wish he had a roommate like I had when I was in school — someone who is around on the weekends to go out with to dinner, to movies, even to the library. It is so much easier to approach people when you're not alone. I also think it's easier for other people to approach you when you're with someone else as well.*
>
> STUDENT REFLECTION

Living with strangers in relatively close quarters can be challenging for anyone, and for the first-year college student, it can sometimes be overwhelming. The expectations of living with someone are sometimes very different from the realities of living with roommates. These issues need to be addressed early on.

Your child's initial expectations about his or her roommate situation (whether chosen or assigned) can set the tone for the entire year. Some students set their expectations too high. They anticipate that their roommates will be their best friends forever. As a result, if roommates don't get along, some students see the situation as catastrophic, which can negatively affect their academic and social life. Other students may see the need to live harmoniously with their roommates, but they develop their real friendships outside the room. They are comfortable with the fact that their roommates do not have to be their best friends.

How each student adjusts to living in a residence hall with roommates is a very individual experience. Respect for others and an appreciation for differences are essential. It is important that students not make assumptions or judgments about a roommate simply because values, behaviors, or appearances may be different from their own. Living with someone from a different culture, ethnic background, or religion can be a learning opportunity that can enrich a student's college experience.

Students bring to college their own unique personality traits, family backgrounds, and coping skills. These factors contribute significantly to how they respond to conditions such as lack of privacy, increased noise, shared bathroom facilities, and constant distractions. For example, a student who has never shared a room before has a lot of adjusting to do with a roommate. Someone who has grown up sharing a bedroom with a sibling may adjust more easily.

Learning how to communicate and compromise is the key to roommate adjustment. It is important for roommates to establish ground rules early in the year. Ground rules might cover issues such as cleaning the room, sharing and borrowing belongings, or dealing with visitors or overnight guests. It is not unusual for a period of politeness to take hold during the first few weeks when everyone is on their best behavior. Usually by about the fourth week, when students are studying for that first exam or writing that first paper, conflicts can develop. Suddenly the loud music or the miscommunication becomes a big deal and can cause tempers to flare. This is the time when students need to revisit how they communicate their needs and how they show respect for another person. As one student told us, "I had to learn to be very open about my feelings to my roommate. If not, problems would escalate past what they had to be."

At most colleges, residence life offices have good support systems in place for students. Hall directors, resident assistants, or student advisers are available in most residence halls to provide leadership and assist in conflict resolution. Floor meetings may be held to help students become aware of housing policies and procedures. Some colleges sponsor roommate adjustment workshops so first-year students can learn how to communicate and cooperate with one another. At many schools, typically during the first month, roommates are required to sign a roommate contract. The contract is established between roommates to ensure that some basic rights and living considerations are observed within each room. The contract addresses issues related to community living such as study and sleep hours, room responsibilities, respect for personal property, and dealing with guests. The contract provides an opportunity for roommates to discuss these issues openly, communicate their individual needs, and generate options and ways to compromise. Once specific details are put in writing, each roommate signs the contract. The fact that students sign the agreement puts responsibility on them for upholding the terms of that contract.

> ❧ *Our daughter had a tough time adjusting to a roommate situation that wasn't working. It's very difficult for a parent to stay uninvolved with the kind of problem she was having. But we did, and our daughter solved it on her own. It took a lot of perseverance on her side, though. It was tough not to be able to solve a problem like she could in the past. We realize it is important for students to work things out with their peers. Just let them know that you care.*

> ❧ *My son's residence adviser was fabulous. He provided some instant help with a roommate problem. Because of this intervention, my son and his roommate have been able to look beyond their differences. They're not best friends, but they get along. At orientation we heard a lot about the role of the residence life staff. We learned from firsthand experience how valuable a good R.A. can be.*
>
> PARENT REFLECTIONS

Here are some important factors for parents to keep in mind when discussing your student's roommate problems.

Strategies for Parents

➽ Good **communication between roommates** is important from the very beginning. Students need to know that it is all right to express their rights, as long as they are not interfering with the rights of others.

➽ Realistic expectations set the tone for a more positive living experience. September is a good time to revisit this topic, which hopefully was discussed sometime during the summer months. If it was not, suggest that **ground rules** be established early on.

➽ Encourage your child to **work through problems** as they arise. A series of misunderstandings may erupt into a major confrontation if tensions are allowed to build.

➽ It is important to remember that **students need to fight their own battles**. The situation can become more complicated when parents get involved in roommate problems.

➥ Whatever the problem, **don't expect an immediate solution**. Often a room change is not an option, and it also does not solve the problem of getting along with others. Taking the time to work through issues can be a positive learning experience.

➥ The office of residence life is experienced in helping students adjust to on-campus living. Suggest that your child make use of resources such as the **resident assistant** (student adviser) or **hall director** (residence director).

COMMUTER SIDEBAR   Students who commute to college from home do not face the challenge of living in a totally new environment; nevertheless, they are presented with their own unique adjustment issues.

First-year college students have new demands placed on them. Adjusting to classes, meeting new people, and possibly trying to fit in part-time job responsibilities can seem overwhelming. The need for many of these students to keep their hometown relationships intact may interfere with their transition to college. Some may get caught up in the lifestyle of friends who have chosen not to go to college and may have more free time. Others may be resistant to making new friends for fear of betraying old ones. How they respond to their campus during that first month can set the framework for their entire collegiate career.

Although you may not experience the same emotions as the parent whose child is living away from home, you need to be aware that changes will take place. Your patience and support during this time are especially important. Although you may see your child every day, you need to realize that things will be different. If you respond to your student's needs as if he or she were still in high school, your child may rebel or even slip back into the high school role.

Strategies for Parents of Commuters

➥ Remember that routines will change. **Schedules may differ** from day to day and include large gaps of free time between classes. Letting your child set his or her own priorities is a good beginning. Your commuter student may find it complicated to get into a rhythm of balancing academics, work, and a social life.

➤➤ Encourage your child to take some risks during the first few weeks of college. Most schools have a **commuter lounge**. Suggest that your son or daughter drop by the lounge once a day to meet other students. This common meeting place can also help the commuter feel as if he or she has a home base. Many lounges have lockers available so students can check their belongings.

➤➤ Early involvement is the key to that first-year connection. Try to brainstorm with your student so he or she will find ways to **get involved**. Even if free time after class is limited, joining one or two organizations can make a difference.

➤➤ Remind your student to **check e-mail messages and the college mailbox** daily. Just because your child lives at home doesn't mean he or she won't receive campus mail. Administrators, professors, and campus clubs use mailboxes, voice mail, and e-mail to communicate important messages to students. In fact, it is not unusual during those first few weeks for student mailboxes to be flooded with information about campus events and activities.

➤➤ Now may be a good time to talk with your child again about personal responsibility. Because of **academic demands**, your student may need to adjust work hours or make different **transportation arrangements**. Your follow-up discussions about finances should focus on the expectations versus the realities of expenses.

> ⥰ *Sometimes my mom gets upset when I'm not home for dinner. She has to understand that there is a lot going on at college.*
> STUDENT REFLECTION

Relationships

> ⥰ *Sometimes it is more "friendsickness" than homesickness. You are so comfortable with your friends that when you go away to college, you long for that feeling again.*
> STUDENT REFLECTION

Developing new relationships while working hard to maintain past ones can be a difficult balancing act for first-year students. In many cases, students and parents are unprepared for the emotional turmoil that changing relationships cause. On one level, your child still has special relationships with former teachers, coaches, guidance counselors, and clergy. On another level, there are high school friends, significant others, and teammates. How and when your child comes to terms with the many changes in these relationships will determine how quickly he or she assimilates into the new college environment.

It is not unusual for a first-year student to seek advice from those who have provided support in the past. For example, initially your student may feel more comfortable sharing feelings with his or her high school counselor than seeking out campus counseling services. Your child might call a former teacher rather than approach a college professor when academics get difficult. This behavior is quite understandable, but if it interferes with your student's ability to make new connections, it can be problematic.

The same is true of peer relationships. Many students have gone through high school, and perhaps their entire childhood, with the same group of friends. Suddenly they find themselves in a situation where they have to learn how to make new friends. As a result, they may try to keep those old relationships alive until they feel comfortable making new ones. Once again, this behavior is understandable, as long as it does not prevent students from making new friends.

Long-distance relationships present their own set of problems. For example, a student who dates someone from home or at another college may visit that person on weekends. During those first crucial weeks, missing campus events and opportunities to meet and bond with peers can have a negative impact. It is during this time that friendships begin to form and relationships take hold.

In order to develop new and meaningful relationships, your student also needs to be open-minded, patient, and willing to take some risks. Rushing to make quick judgments and relying on first impressions can be nonproductive and give your student a narrow and limited perspective of the world. Students who take advantage of opportunities to experience diversity through peer connections will find that they will make new friends and learn to understand differences.

Strategies for Parents

➡ Don't panic if your child initially has difficulty **making connections with peers**. Listen to your child, and affirm his or her efforts.

➡ When appropriate, **encourage your student to take some risks**. Discuss with him or her ways to reach out.

➡ If you are aware that **your student is leaving campus** every weekend, try to find out why. Perhaps opening this issue will spark a good discussion about his or her adjustment to college life.

➤➤ **Don't make premature judgments** about your child's new friends. How you respond can affect how comfortable he or she will feel about sharing things with you in the future.

➤➤ **Getting involved** is a great way to meet new people. Suggest that your student explore clubs, organizations, sports, or special interest groups as a way of making friends. Most colleges provide student handbooks and web sites that contain information about these programs.

> 🐚 *Breaking off a long-term relationship with a boyfriend made the first weeks of school emotionally tumultuous for my daughter. However, worries about roommates melted away, and our daughter quickly bonded with three very diverse and uniquely wonderful young women.*
>
> PARENT REFLECTION

Academic Adjustment

> 🐚 *We got two panic telephone calls. Our daughter felt she didn't belong at the college and should have gone to an "easier school." She said she loved the school, the people, her classes, and her professors, but there was just too much work and not enough hours. Then she'd call the next day, and it would be better. We would hear her out, validate her fears, and encourage her to talk to people at school. She wouldn't talk to staff, but she did talk to peers. Once she realized they were more overwhelmed than she was, she knew she wasn't alone and felt she'd be okay.*
>
> PARENT REFLECTION

The transition from high school to college academics is a major adjustment for most first-year students. Getting accustomed to classes, course preparation, professors, and college exams is no easy task. Regardless of how successful your student was in high school, he or she will have to develop new academic strategies.

You and your student should both be aware of some of the major differences between high school and college academics. Understanding how an academic adviser differs from a high school guidance counselor is a good first step. In high school, the guidance counselor provided a combination of personal and academic assistance. Most colleges separate personal counseling services from academic counseling. Deans' offices and advising centers are designed specifically to focus on academic issues. An academic adviser may be a full-time professional or a member of the faculty. The adviser serves as a coordinator of the student's academic experience by assisting with adding or dropping courses, reviewing short-term academic goals, and recommending appropriate resources.

The next step in academic adjustment may be adapting to a college classroom. The size of the class can be intimidating for some. A large lecture hall can make a student feel isolated or "just a number." A small class can be just as intimidating if the student feels pressured to respond to questions. Note taking, an art in itself, may present new challenges for your student. The teacher, now known as "professor," can initially seem like a larger-than-life figure and thus unapproachable.

Encourage your student to realize that each professor has his or her own unique teaching style. Some may be more lecture oriented, others may involve students in classroom discussions, and others may be less focused and not as organized. The pace of the lecture and the professor's mannerisms and tone of voice will also take some getting used to. Learning how to adapt to different teaching styles can have a positive impact on a student's success in college. One college professor who teaches first-year students offers this advice: "In some cases, a student might have to adapt to these differences in styles in as little time as the ten to fifteen minutes between classes. It is important that students are flexible in responding to the differences and not tune out faculty who use less preferred teaching styles."

Some introductory courses may be frustrating to your student if these courses don't meet his or her expectations. For example, your student may think that Psychology 101 will be about working with people and learning about different personality traits. In fact, most introductory psychology courses require students to spend a considerable amount of time memorizing psychological and physiological terms.

For many students, their first test or quiz brings home the fact that they are no longer in high school. They are surprised to find that what contributed to their success in the past does not always work for them in college. Their frustrations may even cause them to question whether they are attending the right college. Students need to evaluate their study habits and reassess the amount of time they devote to course and test preparation. Urge your student to talk with the professor about his or her academic performance. That first test is a good springboard for discussion and can make talking to a professor more comfortable for your child.

Setting priorities and taking responsibility for decisions are important for your child to do, especially when they relate to new-found freedoms.

For example, policies on class attendance vary from institution to institution. Some colleges require students to attend all classes, and others may be less rigid. The freedom to cut classes makes setting priorities and taking responsibility even more important.

Strategies for Parents

➨ **Approaching a professor** for the first time can be an intimidating experience. Suggest that your child talk to a resident assistant or observe other students chatting with a professor. This may make it easier for your son or daughter to have that first discussion with a professor.

➨ Students should be aware of the **office locations and office hours** of their professors. Most professors make this information available during the first week of classes.

➨ If your child is confused about the **specific requirements of a course**, refer him or her to the course syllabus. Students frequently put the syllabus in the back of their notebook and forget about it. Remind your student that a course syllabus contains important information about course content, specific dates, and deadlines for assignments and exams.

➨ Remember that times change! Be careful about **giving advice based on your own college experience**. What worked for you some years ago (study habits, approach to courses, exam preparation) may not be effective for your son or daughter.

➨ Just as **teaching styles** vary for professors, so do **learning styles** differ among students. Encourage your child to seek out some resources that will reveal how he or she learns best.

➨ If your child shares some concerns with you, don't get into **the trap of blaming the professor**. Ask *who, what, where, when,* and *why* questions to see the bigger picture.

➨ If your child is ready to change a major or drop a class because of a poor grade on a first test, urge him or her not to overreact. Suggest **talking to the professor or adviser to explore options**.

➨ Place the responsibility on your student for connecting with resources at the first sign of academic trouble. Students should reach out to **campus support services** such as tutorials, advisers, and deans.

Apprehensions may set in. Your child would not have been accepted to college if he or she did not possess the abilities and skills to achieve academic success. Remind your student of this. Your son or daughter should remember that it is normal to feel somewhat inadequate at this time.

Coping with New Freedoms

> *This was my first child leaving home, and I was worried. I kept telling myself that I had spent eighteen years instilling in him good values and a good work ethic, and I had to be confident that he would continue to work hard and make responsible decisions.*
>
> PARENT REFLECTION

As your student begins to settle into new surroundings, he or she will be faced with many choices that may test his or her values and cause him or her to question previous decisions. Questions may arise about sex, religion, politics, personal beliefs, or the greater worldview. Your student's past experiences, level of maturity, family ties, and coping skills play an important part in how he or she responds to new-found freedoms. Whom students choose to spend their time with and how they decide to spend their time may reflect the changes they are making in the way they view themselves in their new world.

Once at college, students may find themselves with people or in situations that represent an entirely different set of personal values. Deciding where they fit in, without compromising their sense of self, is a key developmental task for first-year students. At this point, peer pressure can take on a whole new meaning. For example, your child and someone in the same residence hall may decide to attend an off-campus party together where alcohol will be served. Although your child may have avoided this type of partying in the past, right now his or her need to fit in is more important. Hopefully, as your student becomes more comfortable in this new environment, he or she will make choices that are more compatible with core, personal values.

This need to fit in may also drive your student to look for new outlets of self-expression. You may notice some changes in your student's appearance — a different hair color (even one not found in nature, like green or blue), a different style of clothing, body piercing, tattoos — that can be interpreted as signs of independence, rebellion, or risk taking. Your student's language may change (more slang, profanity), as well as his or her choice of music or food preferences.

Newly found freedoms can sometimes result in students making careless decisions that can put them at odds with the college. Violations of the campus alcohol policy, for example, may result in disciplinary action against the student. Going to bars, leaving parties with strangers, walking alone at night, or pairing off with someone he or she just met are risky behaviors that can jeopardize a student's personal safety. The inability to connect behavior with consequences can make students vulnerable to physical assault, sexual assault, and robbery.

Strategies for Parents

➤ Don't overreact to changes. Ask questions, but don't jump to conclusions. **Convey your trust**. The more you attempt to understand the world of your student, the better prepared you will be to respond to these changes.

➤ Risk taking is an entirely new experience for some students. Sometime during this month, revisit some earlier conversations with your child that focused on **sexual assault, substance abuse, and safety measures**.

➤ In an effort to be accepted and to be with others, students can get into a **cycle of drinking**. Brainstorm with your son or daughter about what else the campus has to offer: activities, sporting events, clubs, performances.

➤ Ask questions about how your child is **spending free time** and whom he or she is spending it with. The way your child spends free time can give clues as to whether he or she is engaging in risky activities.

➤ Notice your child's **spending patterns**. Does money seem to evaporate overnight? Is there more money available than there should be? Changes in your child's spending patterns may signal involvement in drugs or alcohol.

➤ Now might be a good time to remind your son or daughter about **security resources** such as shuttles, campus escort systems, and emergency telephones. Students who have cell phones should remember to bring them along when they go out.

➤ Colleges do not watch students twenty-four hours a day. Parents, as well as students, need to **be aware of college policies and regulations** that can be found in most student handbooks.

Fraternities and Sororities

Many students are attracted to the possibility of joining a college fraternity or sorority and participating in Greek life. They are drawn to the sense of community, spirit, and common goals that chapter members share. They also may view joining this organization as an opportunity to establish their identity within a specific group.

There are many advantages to a sorority or fraternity membership. Members learn leadership skills by organizing events, getting involved in committees, and serving on executive boards. They often participate in community service and philanthropic experiences, affiliate with local and national chapters, maintain alumni connections, and sometimes enjoy living in a fraternity or sorority house. Since students are required to maintain certain academic standards, membership can have a positive effect on scholastic achievement.

Membership recruitment is commonly known as "rushing." During this time, usually in the fall or spring of the first or second year, prospective members receive information about the chapter and are invited to attend informal and formal sessions to meet current members. Most sororities and fraternities sponsor dry rush parties (no alcohol) as part of their recruitment process. At the end of this process, selected students are invited to engage in membership activities (pledging).

Pledging, which may be referred to by other names, generally takes place within a concentrated period of time. Students are educated about the history, mission, and goals of the chapter and presented with opportunities and activities designed to help them bond and create a sense of community. At the end of this period, students who meet the criteria will be invited to become chapter members.

Parents and students should be well informed about the many aspects of Greek life. You should ask questions about finances early in the process. Most chapters require membership dues, and new members are expected to pay a one-time initiation fee. You should find out how the cost of living in a fraternity or sorority house compares with the cost of living in other campus housing facilities.

Parents and students should try to find out as much as possible about the chapter's reputation, the composition of the membership, and, more specifically, the organization's initiation rituals and traditions. National attention has focused on initiation rituals commonly known as hazing, which is any behavior that willfully and recklessly endangers the physical or mental health of an individual. What students may think of as innocent or harmless pranks or stunts can lead to disaster and tragedy. As a result, most states have antihazing laws. Colleges also have guidelines against hazing that include disciplinary procedures and sanctions that will be imposed on offenders. For some specific guidelines on how to address hazing issues, you may want to refer to the list of web sites in Appendix C.

Parents and students should be well aware of the kinds of programs and events sponsored by the chapter. Some may have a greater emphasis on social service and community action programs, while others may have a broader mission. Pay particular attention to the kinds of social activities offered during the year. Parents should have their son or daughter explore the reputation of the chapter and its members. Those involved with excessive partying, alcohol infractions, and other personal safety risks should be avoided.

If your child has expressed an interest in participating in Greek life, encourage him or her to look at the big picture and consider how the membership will affect his or her total college experience. Consider the effect that membership will have on peer relationships, individual and group identity, and time commitments. As a parent, your support, your ability to listen, and your insights will go a long way in helping your student through this process.

> *I worried when my daughter told me she was interested in joining a sorority. I've read some upsetting stories about hazing activities on college campuses. But I was pleased that my daughter really did her homework. She decided against choosing a sorority that her friends joined and chose one that better suited her. It has all worked out very well. She feels part of a group and has become very involved in causes for the homeless. This was a community outreach program which was adopted by her sorority last year. In fact, her involvement has led her to rethink her career path. She has kept her English major but has picked up a minor in human services.*
>
> PARENT REFLECTION

Time Management

> *The one concern that our daughter communicated to us was her need to come to grips with time management issues. All of a sudden, there was no parental direction or suggestion about what time to be home, when to do homework, go to bed, and so on. Therefore, she would — and still does — call home complaining about always being tired and not getting enough rest.*
>
> PARENT REFLECTION

Time Management

We all work by the same clock — twenty-four hours a day, seven days a week — but how we manage that time is a very individual process. Students can become easily overwhelmed balancing an academic schedule, learning to live in a new environment, and establishing a social life. A major challenge for your child at this time is learning how to set priorities and stick to them.

Students now find themselves in an environment in which there is no one to tell them when to get up, when to go to bed, when to study, or when to come home. How your student initially responds to new freedoms can have a positive or a negative impact on his or her college experience. In fact, studies on first-year college students repeatedly identify good time management practices as a factor that can contribute to student success. Here's what some sophomores had to say about this issue as they reflected on their experience as first-year students.

> *As far as time management goes, I think that's every freshman's downfall. I made terrible grades last year, and I think many other people did too. Part of the problem, of course, is learning how to juggle a new social situation with new academic pressures. But also, you just haven't learned the tricks yet. I learned eventually that I simply couldn't take a class before 10 A.M. if I expected to go to it. I learned that the best time for me to study was before going out on Friday and Saturday nights, from about 7 P.M. to 10 P.M. It takes awhile to get into a rhythm. I found mine second semester this year. And then it becomes really fun — at least it did for me, because I had a great sense of having it all — a fun social life and good grades.*

> *Pace yourself! Start by doing the homework and reading as soon as possible. Don't fall behind like I did. You may never catch up.*

> *Learning to work with blocks of time during the day was really tough in the beginning. Even if I had three hours between classes, I wouldn't start studying until after dinner. I was still on high school time rather than college time. The best thing happened when I went to a time management workshop with my roommate. I learned to find what worked for me. Now if I have a lot of time between classes, I try to use some of that time to review my notes. This gives me more time in the evening to study and to get more involved with the campus radio station, which I really enjoy.*

STUDENT REFLECTIONS

When the first semester begins, students need to renew the good time management skills that they used in high school. Then they need to make adjustments to old patterns and be open to new time management skills. Good time management strategies such as wearing a watch, setting an alarm clock, making to-do lists, and using planners or date books are things that students often take for granted. Once school begins and the pace becomes hectic, these strategies will be major building blocks for developing new routines.

There are two categories of time wasters: internal and external. Internal time wasters are things such as procrastination, the inability to say no, and starting projects but never finishing them. Students have control of these internal time wasters. External time wasters are things such as incoming telephone calls, constant interruptions, and computer problems. They are controlled by the environment and outside circumstances. Parents can play a key role in helping students identify time wasters that interfere with the way they use their time. Some of the following strategies might be especially helpful.

Strategies for Parents

▶▶ Remember that some **internal time wasters** may be a part of your child's personality and will always be present. Remind your student that there are ways to work with these issues so that they will not hamper academic progress.

▶▶ Be prepared to listen to frustrations about your student's inability to estimate time: the time needed to study for a test, prepare a paper, or get to and from classes. It will take time and patience for your son or daughter to get into a **time management** rhythm.

▶▶ Recommend that your child look for **places on campus that are conducive to study**. Everyone's needs are different, so what works for one student might not work for another.

▶▶ Encourage your student to **seek out campus resources** that can assist him or her with new coping strategies. Tutorial programs, counseling services, and academic advisers can be especially helpful in addressing time wasters.

▶▶ Remember that it is your student who needs to take responsibility for managing his or her own time. Attempting to organize your child's time can often complicate matters. However, as a parent, you can provide some **helpful tips** — for example:

➤➤ **Break down large tasks** into smaller, more manageable ones. This can help your student feel less overwhelmed and helps reduce the tendency to procrastinate.

➤➤ **Schedule difficult tasks during high-energy times**. For example, if your child is a morning person, he or she will accomplish more before noon than late in the evening.

➤➤ Take advantage of **blocks of free time** between classes. Class preparation and studying do not have to be put on hold until the end of the day.

➤➤ Use an **academic planner** to manage a schedule that focuses on course work first. Establish a balance between academics and social or extracurricular activities.

Validating Your Feelings

🐚 *While we had a difficult time with our daughter leaving, a younger sibling especially missed her. He wanted to call her the night we moved her in and did so frequently during the next few days. Letting go and not worrying (as much!) has been difficult for the whole family.*

PARENT REFLECTION

You have been very busy preparing your child for all the changes that college brings. Now it is time to sit back, reward yourself for all your hard work, and deal with your own emotions. Negative feelings may come and go with very little warning as you possibly go through self-doubt, anger, guilt, fear, loss, or confusion. Many things may trigger your emotions: aromas of your college student's favorite meal, music from a special song, or your dog's forlorn look.

You may find that you are preoccupied with finances. No matter how well you planned for your child's education, the costs can seem overwhelming. Tuition payments, loan payments, and spending money for your student all represent financial responsibilities that add to your stress.

Feelings of separation and loss are unique to each individual. The relationship between you and your child will affect the intensity of those feelings. For example, if you spent a great deal of time with your son or daughter, you probably will feel a greater sense of loss. On the other hand, if your contact with your child was limited to brief encounters between comings and goings, you may have a more delayed reaction to his or her

Separation and Loss

absence. Your reactions may also be affected by your child's gender or standing in the family (youngest, oldest, middle, or only child).

The distance between home and college can have a powerful emotional impact on many parents. Just knowing that your college student is a car ride away can provide you with a level of comfort. Greater distances are often harder to deal with and serve to emphasize your student's absence and independence. The need for parent and student to agree on regular channels of communication takes on great importance.

For parents who are sending a child away to college for the first time, their feelings of excitement, pride, and anticipation can often be overshadowed by intense feelings of sadness and anxiety. If you are a first-timer, be sure you do not transfer your feelings on to your son or daughter. Some parents may feel a sense of relief when their last child ventures off to college, while others may feel uncomfortable in their empty-nest environment.

> *There were many emotions. This is my second and last child going to college. My husband and I were facing the empty nest. We were a little nervous, and sometimes excited. Then I'd feel guilty for looking forward to it. I was sad and emotional and trying to hold on to my daughter.*
>
> PARENT REFLECTION

Different family make-ups such as one-parent families, divorced or separated parents, or households with stepchildren, all present their own unique challenges and can produce a complex set of emotions. These parents may experience more ambivalence because of the complicated nature of their relationship with their child. Families need to be reassured that there is no one way to respond. It is important that they own their feelings and consider looking for avenues that will allow them to work through them. Sometimes just talking to a friend or other parents in similar situations can help to reduce anxieties.

> *As a single mom with only one child, I truly went through an emotional time when my son was preparing to enter college. It has always been just the two of us since he was a year old, and although I knew he was independent and ready for this experience, I also knew I would have a difficult time. I was proud of his accomplishments and maturity and readiness, but I also wanted to hold on to him as tightly as possible. I also wanted him to have a great college experience.*
>
> PARENT REFLECTION

Changes in family routines can be a vivid reminder that your child is no longer at home. The day-to-day activities within the home can take on an entirely new look for siblings and parents alike. Daily chores might need to be reassigned to other members of the family. Familiar rituals such as attendance at sporting events or weekly music lessons might be discontinued altogether. Routines that once provided balance to your life are now disrupted. Your ability to cope probably will be greatly tested. In one sense, you are trying to get a better handle on your own emotions at the same time you are trying to provide sound, practical advice to your first-year student.

Monthly Checklist: Managing Emotions

☑ Give yourself a pat on the back for getting through September. Surviving the first month is a major accomplishment, so congratulate yourself!

☑ Accept your ambivalent feelings. It's okay to feel torn between excitement and sadness.

☑ Don't overreact to problems. If your anxious student detects panic in your voice, it may heighten his or her emotional response. Emotions can be contagious.

☑ If you're dealing with the empty-nest syndrome, take some action. Spend some time reflecting on who you are and what is important to you. Explore possible new activities, and identify formal and informal support systems.

☑ Remember that if you are feeling some sense of loss, other members of your household probably are too. Some may be more comfortable sharing feelings than others. Pay close attention to the behavioral cues of younger siblings. They may need extra support at this time.

The Balancing Act

October and November

October

November

🙿 *I thought once I got through September, things would be a bit easier, and in some ways they are. I know my way around campus, and I've started to hang out with a group of guys on my floor. My biggest problem right now is trying to fit everything in. It's hard to sort out what's important and what I need to do first. I really want to get involved in student government like I did in high school, but I have so much reading to keep up with. I guess I need to learn how to plan a schedule and stick to it.*

FIRST-YEAR STUDENT

You and your student have both survived the first month of college. The newness has worn off, and the telephone calls probably aren't quite as frantic. Now it's time to focus on communication: asking questions without being intrusive, expressing concerns without preaching, and just showing that you care. October and November is the time when students have to set the right priorities and make academic decisions. Communicating with

COMMUTER SIDEBAR Commuter students often find that they have to make some extra effort to become involved in campus activities. In the long run, these efforts really pay off. If staying on campus after classes is not possible, they might want to think about using blocks of time between classes to become involved. For example, playing on an intramural team or joining a club that meets at a specific time during the day may be a good choice. Remind your commuter student to read bulletin boards, campus web pages, and the student newspaper regularly to find out what is going on.

them during these months, as well as during family weekend and Thanksgiving break may be challenging.

OCTOBER and NOVEMBER ISSUES

Student Issues

1. I'm still adjusting. Sometimes it gets lonely here. There are times when I'd like to just go home for the evening.

2. I need to plan a weekend to go home.

3. My long-distance relationships are starting to fade a bit.

4. Mid-semester exams are coming up soon. I'm worried about them.

5. It's hard to balance academics and extracurricular activities.

6. There are still a lot of social pressures, like alcohol and fitting in.

7. My grades aren't what I expected them to be. Did I come to the right college?

8. I wonder if my money is going to stretch far enough.

9. I wish I could go home in time to help prepare for Thanksgiving.

10. Family Weekend is coming up. I'm a little nervous about my parents being here.

11. I've never lived with so much diversity. I'm still adjusting to that.

Parent Issues

1. My child is coming home for the first visit. It kind of makes me nervous because I want everything to be right.

2. Family Weekend is coming up. I'm a little nervous about being on campus with my child.

3. The family dynamic is still so different. I wonder when it will balance out.

4. I'm worried that my student is not studying enough for midsemester exams.

5. Thanksgiving will be different this year. One member of the family will just be visiting. How can I make it memorable?

Setting the Right Priorities

Now that your student has survived the first month of college and is somewhat settled in, the newness of college will begin to wear off. Your student now will be confronted with the reality and demands of course work, tests, and papers. He or she has also had a chance to become familiar with most campus clubs or activities. Deciding what to join, with whom to join, and how much time to invest in them requires some deliberate planning. In their need to belong, it is not unusual for enthusiastic first-year students to overextend themselves. In their quest to meet new people, they might become so engrossed in a whirlwind of social activities that academics become less of a priority. Learning how to balance their time often becomes a challenge. Some students have trouble prioritizing. Distractions because of roommate issues, concerns about high school friends, and peer acceptance can all contribute to students expending a tremendous amount of time and energy. Making good decisions about what needs immediate attention, what kind of action to take, and what resources to connect with can go a long way in helping students to set priorities.

> *It can all be so overwhelming. But you have to make a choice; you can continue to feel overwhelmed or set up a plan. I would make up a list of activities for the week, and when the time came, I would see if I could fit them all in.*
>
> STUDENT REFLECTION

Continue to show your support by suggesting different ways of managing their time.

Relationships with roommates may be flourishing, or perhaps they are filled with conflict. Regardless of the situation, your son or daughter will probably expend a great deal of energy working on a harmonious living situation. The period of politeness may be over, and differences that neophyte roommates previously ignored are now out in the open, perhaps causing tension and conflict. The stress that accompanies an uncomfortable living situation usually overshadows a student's academic and social life. Some students put a lot of energy into working things out themselves, while others may seek out campus resources such as counseling or residence staff to assist them. Other students may request a room change, which may or may not be possible.

Some students, in an effort to hold on to old relationships, may travel to other colleges to visit high school friends. They also may be spending an

Roommates

excessive amount of time communicating by telephone or e-mail, all of which can prevent them from feeling academically and socially connected to their new setting.

The need for peer acceptance can sometimes interfere with the ability to make sound judgments. It may even cause your student to engage in inappropriate behaviors or activities that may result in severe consequences. A student's decision to consume alcohol as a means of fitting in can affect both the quality and quantity of energy he or she puts into academics. It can have such an impact on behavior that it may result in college disciplinary action. Setting the wrong priorities during these first few months can establish habits and patterns of behavior that can be hard to break. For example, some students decide that weekends begin on Wednesday or Thursday evenings, and as a result, they cut classes the next day.

As a parent, you will probably try to get a sense of what is going on, what priorities your child has set, and how your student is spending time. Knowing the right kinds of questions to ask can open up communication. Expressing concerns without sounding judgmental is part of the balancing act you may experience.

It's All in How You Say It

Although September may have involved daily contact, frantic telephone calls, and unintelligible messages left on the answering machine, October and November bring a noticeable change in the communication patterns between students and parents. The frequency of calls may change, the intensity of the conversations may vary, and complaints usually begin to level off.

> *If they are unhappy the first few months, don't overreact. Encourage them to allow time to adjust to this new lifestyle. Give them the freedom to make their own decisions, but encourage them not to decide prematurely.*
>
> PARENT REFLECTION

Some students are naturally more forthcoming than others with information. They describe daily activities, share new experiences, and express concerns. Others volunteer very little. In fact, their responses to most questions may be limited to "yes," "no," and "fine." An attempt to elicit a response to even a simple question about school progress can result in a stressful encounter.

🐚 *It's difficult not knowing what they do with their time and also not knowing what they do with their money. We've had some frank discussions with our son about his spending habits. We decided to provide him with money once a month so he can learn to budget, and while he admits that it is hard to do, he has managed to make independent decisions about his finances.*

PARENT REFLECTION

Now that many homes and workplaces have computers, communication by e-mail has become more commonplace. This form of communication has its pros and cons. It can be valuable because it provides a continuous connection, and it is less expensive and more convenient than the telephone. However, it does have its drawbacks. The nature of the exchange is different since conversations tend to be shorter and emotional overtones are hard to discern.

Whatever form of communication you use, be aware that how you ask questions can be as important as the questions themselves. The following strategies might help you establish a healthy, ongoing dialogue between you and your child.

Strategies for Parents

➤ Try not to rely on just one form of communication. Although e-mail is easy, it can be less personal than the telephone. There is nothing like **hearing a familiar voice** from time to time.

➤ Establish **a telephone call routine**. Identify certain days and times to connect with one another. An occasional card or letter is also a nice touch.

➤ Keep things in perspective. Try to **be a sounding board** rather than a critic. This keeps the door open for both good and bad news.

➤ **Good listening is an art**. Interrupting, finishing your student's sentences, and firing off questions does not encourage an ongoing dialogue.

➤ Even if your child has made some poor decisions, **try not to place blame** directly on him or her. Using *I* statements rather than *you* statements allows you to express how you feel without sounding accusatory: *"When you stay out all night instead of doing homework, I worry about your grades."* vs. *"You've got to stop staying out all night with your friends."*

➡ Lack of information can sometimes cause you to make **inaccurate assumptions**. Try to find out what is going on before jumping to conclusions.

➡ Asking **open-ended questions**, such as "How did that feel?" or "What do you think?" encourages communication and avoids superficial answers. For example, if you want to find out about eating habits, you might ask, "What did you have for lunch?" rather than "Are you eating enough?"

➡ **Work on controlling your emotions**. Feelings of anger and disappointment will come through even on the telephone.

➡ **Stay away from clichés** such as, "I know how you feel," "These are the best days of your life," or "It can't be that bad." These phrases don't necessarily represent the empathy you may want to convey. Instead you might say, "I am sorry you feel this way. I don't know how to help, but I'm here to listen," or "Why not tell me a little bit about what's been going on, and maybe we can problem-solve together."

➡ Be aware that strong words expressed in an **e-mail can have a powerful impact**. They can be downloaded, printed, and thus become permanent.

COMMUTER SIDEBAR The balancing act for many commuters can be quite complicated because they may have less control over setting their own priorities. A student who carpools with other students may not be able to hang around campus when classes are over, and a student with an off-campus job may have to adjust his or her schedule to coincide with work commitments. Brainstorming options or suggesting possible compromises with your child can be an important role for a parent of a commuter. For example, if the college has a commuter club, you might suggest that your student inquire about the availability of a listing of other commuter students who may also be interested in carpooling. In some cases, having a few options can provide more flexibility to your child's schedule.

🐌 *I am a "Velcro parent" in that I throw questions at my son when I call him and hang on to every word. But my son "un-Velcros" me right away with his responses. I know I have crossed the line when his answers are reduced to just "yes," "no," and "fine."*

      The only thing that elicited any kind of a response was when he failed his first test in a difficult subject. He called me at work, so I knew he was nervous about it. He really wanted to do well."

                                                      Parent Reflections

Academic Decision Making

During October and November, your student will be thrust into the reality of college academics. Grades from tests and papers, deadlines, and midsemester exams can all contribute to student stress. It can also be an unsettling time for parents.

    Midsemester exams can be a major source of anxiety for many first-year students. Although some students already have feedback on their progress in a specific course, others may not know their academic status in a course until after the midsemester exams. Knowing what to anticipate for the exam, dealing with a volume of information, and planning and organizing study times are all common student concerns. Even if your child was a confident, well-prepared high school student, don't be surprised if your student now questions his or her ability and expresses self-doubt.

      Our daughter was a bit overwhelmed keeping up with the required reading. The Introduction to Psychology course she is finding very tough. I've advised her to approach her professor, but I don't think she has yet. Learning how to manage her time better will be a huge goal to accomplish.

                                                      Parent Reflection

Encourage your child to talk to professors or teaching assistants. Many students find it easiest to stay after class and talk briefly with professors first to break the ices. After that, making an appointment may be more comfortable for your child.

    Hopefully, your student realized fairly soon after the first major test that what contributed to success in high school may not be as effective in college. If your child is not getting the anticipated academic results, he or she may need to readjust course strategies. For example, using flash cards to study for a multiple-choice test might be better than simply rereading the chapter and reviewing notes. Or your first-year student may find that

Midsemester Exams

discussing course material in a study group will make the information more relevant than just sitting alone and memorizing terms.

A visit to tutorial services can help your child assess changes that might need to be made. For example, students may become aware of different learning patterns — learning by example, repeatedly reviewing content, remembering content by linking practical experiences to it — that will contribute to positive changes in their approach to course work. Personalizing the learning experience can help students feel more in control of their academic life.

At many colleges, students are expected to register for second-semester classes sometime during November. The registration process differs from institution to institution. Some colleges require students to contact an academic adviser prior to registration, others preregister students; and still others provide students with information over the Internet and allow for telephone registration. Whatever the process might be, students must be aware of registration deadlines. In many cases, first-year students do not get the ideal schedule that they had hoped for. For example, it is not unusual for them to be assigned the latest registration times, which often means they end up with their second or third choice of classes and a less popular class time. Although this process can cause considerable student anxiety, it is a real part of life on a college campus.

Choosing a major is another issue that your student may have to address at this time. Many students do not have to declare an academic discipline until their sophomore or junior year. They do, however, need to begin thinking about the decision-making process. Now is the time for your student to gather information about the various disciplines offered at his or her college. Since your student may confuse choosing a major with choosing a career, it is important that he or she receive sound information from the very beginning. For example, most career centers can help students narrow down areas of interests and help them focus on their abilities and identify their values. During this process of self-assessment, students can begin exploring possible majors through specific course selections and ongoing conversations with academic advisers and professors.

Some students who began college with a major in mind may now begin to question that decision. For some, questioning their choice may be premature, but for others it may be very appropriate. For example, the chemistry major who fails her first big chemistry exam should not consider this as an indication that the major is too difficult. She should instead evaluate how she prepared for the exam. On the other hand, the psychology major who finds the subject matter boring and may have done poorly on the exam probably does need to reevaluate the choice of major. In any case, it is important that these students receive assistance and support when reviewing academic choices. Career planning offices, academic advising, and counseling services can serve as valuable resources at this time.

October and November represent significant academic challenges to first-year students. Although parents may justifiably feel a sense of pride at their child's accomplishments, they may also feel a sense of helplessness as they try to help their student cope and understand his or her decisions. Some parents find it difficult to resist the temptation to rush in and fix everything.

> 🕮 *My daughter called one day and said, "I want to transfer to another school." I was surprised and immediately asked her, "What would you study there?" When she said accounting, I was shocked. She had been set on becoming a teacher since she was a little girl, and I knew the school she had in mind to transfer to didn't have an education program. I gently reminded her to think it over and that we'd talk about it in a few days. I hesitated calling her, but when we spoke, she didn't even bring it up. I finally said, "So did you think more about transferring?" She said, "Oh, Mom, I'm not transferring."*
>
> PARENT REFLECTION

It is not always easy to sit back and just listen, but sometimes pausing to think about the idea is just the answer. Students need to take responsibility for their own problem solving, decision making, and seeking out resources. You can assist in this process by expressing support and encouragement.

Strategies for Parents

➺ **Stress** can interfere with your child's ability to focus or concentrate on the task at hand. Encourage your son or daughter to think about what has worked in the past. Some effective "stress busters" are exercise, listening to music, and artistic expression.

➺ **Test anxiety**, which can interfere with academic performance, is not always easy to identify. If your student feels prepared but still is not getting the desired results, maybe it is time to touch base with a counselor. As a parent, you might gently recommend this resource. You can provide your child with the appropriate telephone number, but it is important that he or she make the call.

➤➤ If **midsemester grades** are distributed and you have questions about parent access, you should review issues concerning the Buckley Amendment (FERPA).

➤➤ If your child is having **academic difficulty**, provide some help by identifying tutorial programs on campus. Support networks might include tutorial centers, peer study groups sponsored by academic departments, web sites, and tutorial programs sponsored by residence halls.

➤➤ Don't overreact if your student makes a frantic plea for help with the registration process. This cry for help may come as a worrisome telephone call or a stress-filled e-mail. At most colleges, **an ideal schedule is often impossible** for first-year students. If your child has significant concerns, suggest that he or she talk to an academic adviser.

➤➤ **Choosing a major** is a process that takes time. It may be difficult not to step in and choose a major for your child. Encourage your student to explore academic programs, but do not project your own views into the process. Remember that a student's choice of a major is based on his or her abilities and interests, not yours.

Family Weekend

Many colleges sponsor a family weekend for first-year students, usually in October or early November (though sometimes in the spring). A common goal of these programs is to provide an opportunity for parents to interact with their student in the college environment. Unlike a high school open house where parents and teachers discuss academic performance, this weekend allows you to observe and experience your student's new world.

To help parents plan for the weekend, some colleges offer hotel and meal packages. Some sponsor very formal structured activities, while others offer more informal gatherings with lots of free time. There may be an academic component to the weekend as well, which may include a faculty presentation or an opportunity to sit in on classes. Most programs offer an array of cultural and social activities, including sporting events, musical programs, receptions, dinners, and art exhibits. Some provide religious services and opportunities to attend special community events.

Probably by now your child has become accustomed to some of the major challenges in his or her new environment. In fact, you may be surprised at how quickly your student has changed. Depending on the distance from home to college, you may have had an opportunity already to observe these changes firsthand. Some parents enthusiastically look forward to this first campus event to check out their student's progress. You may notice some differences in your child from the very first moment you set foot on campus. Your college student may already be more confident, taking on the role of a host for the weekend.

What takes place during this weekend may be quite different from what you expected. For example, you may be looking forward to spending some special moments alone with your child, but he or she may have already invited roommates, friends, and their parents to join you. You may want to attend a specific program, but your student might be more interested in sleeping in that morning. Although agendas and needs may differ, the success of your visit will greatly depend on your patience, flexibility, and understanding.

COMMUTER SIDEBAR Commuter students sometimes feel that family weekend events are just for students who live on campus. Remember, though, that attendance at this kind of program is another way for both you and your child to feel more connected to the college. If participating in the entire program is not possible, discuss with your commuter student a few activities that you might want to attend together.

> *We were glad that we arranged beforehand to have some private time together with our daughter during the weekend. It was important because everything seemed to be built around everyone being together: parents, friends, roommates.*
>
> Parent Reflection

Separated, divorced, or remarried parents need to be sensitive to a number of issues. Who gets invited to what events may depend on the college's database, as well as the dynamics within the family. There could be many awkward moments when a parent suddenly shows up with a new spouse. Nevertheless, the focus of the weekend needs to be on the student, not on who goes to what event with whom. Clear communication and good planning are important in this situation.

Strategies for Parents

➤➤ If parent relationships are strained, try not to put your child in the middle of the conflict. Be open and flexible about plans, and be willing to compromise. Try to work out issues before you attend the **family weekend** program.

➤➤ Do your homework. **Make hotel and restaurant reservations** well in advance. Poor planning can be stressful and may put a damper on your weekend.

➤➤ Don't get so involved in the weekend's events that you miss important **cues in your child's behavior**. Be aware that there may be issues concerning academics, adjustment, or homesickness that he or she may hesitate to discuss with you.

➤➤ Be open to changes. Don't be surprised to see your student wearing clothes that you've never seen before or a roommate wearing clothes you may have purchased. There may be some **new behaviors and mannerisms** that might catch you off-guard.

➤➤ If there are problems, don't look to the family weekend for a quick fix. The focus of the program will determine what kind of questions you can address. Don't expect to get answers to important questions if **some school offices are not open** over the weekend.

➤➤ Don't forget to **bring care packages**. Your child will appreciate snacks, hometown newspapers, and money. Be prepared to go shopping.

➤➤ **Saying good-bye** at the end of the weekend may be difficult for everyone. Validate your child's feelings and reinforce your support. Encourage your student to get back into a routine.

➤➤ The college may have some **special activities for younger siblings**. Ask about these activities or check into community resources that may be available for younger children.

Thanksgiving Break — The First Big Holiday

Although some schools have a fall break, Thanksgiving is usually the first major holiday when students typically go home. Whether your student spends this holiday at home probably depends on travel time, travel expenses, and class schedules. Most colleges provide a four-day Thanksgiving break. Because of the high number of travelers at this time, be sure to make airline, train, or bus reservations well in advance.

The anticipation of returning home for the holiday can stir up powerful emotions for both parent and student. As a parent, you may find yourself particularly nostalgic and reflective at this time. If preparing for the holiday was typically a family affair, you may feel a sense of sadness and loss if your college student is not home for the initial planning stage. If Thanksgiving is the first opportunity your child has had to visit home, your feelings of excitement may be mixed with anxiety about how he or she may have changed.

Your son or daughter may also be wondering what changes have taken place at home, particularly if there have been few or no opportunities for a weekend visit until now. Students often hope that their bedroom is just as they left it, or they may be wondering if the dog will still jump all over them with excitement. Students are sometimes anxious about answering relatives' questions about how things are going, especially if the adjustment process has not progressed as smoothly as they had hoped. For the self-conscious first-year student, well-meaning questions or comments can cause considerable anxiety. For example, a simple question such as, "So how do you like living in the dorm?" may trigger an uncomfortable, emotional response if the student is having significant roommate problems.

Parent and student expectations may be quite different. Although your child may be eagerly waiting for a home-cooked turkey dinner with all the trimmings, chances are that the number-one priority will be to connect with high school friends. And although you know how important friends are, you may be expecting to have some quality time alone with your son or daughter before school starts up again. In some instances, you may get that special time with your child. Many parents report, however, that they simply couldn't keep up with their student's comings and goings during the break.

It is not unusual for students to spend a lot of time with old friends, comparing notes about each other's college experiences. They may talk about food, roommates, classes, and social activities. In most cases, students are relieved to find that high school relationships are still intact. Some, however, may begin to note some changes in their friends, which can be a bit unsettling. Even minor changes such as preferences in food or music can serve as a reminder that things are no longer the same.

> ❧ *Our son's first Thanksgiving home we bumped into both the "boy we've missed you" issue and the curfew issue. We could hardly wait to see him. He had not been home since he left in August. He was very happy to do the parent/sister thing for an hour and then was immediately on the phone to round up all the buddies he hadn't seen and had only e-mailed in the fall. The curfew was*

really my issue. I could not get to sleep unless I knew he was at home and safe. He did not want a curfew but also understood my need. We agreed on a time for curfew over Thanksgiving that met both our needs.

PARENT REFLECTION

Strategies for Parents

➤➤ Try to maintain **holiday traditions** that are important to your family. Nevertheless, some preparations might have to be put on hold until your college student arrives home. Be flexible.

➤➤ If you are divorced or separated, try to **have holiday plans worked out in advance** so your child doesn't feel caught in the middle. Communicate concerns before your child arrives home.

➤➤ Be realistic about the amount of time you expect your child to spend at home. For many first-year students, this is **a time to renew high school friendships** in an effort to alleviate fears that things have changed.

➤➤ Communicate, but don't pump your student with questions. Remember, **it's all in how you say it**.

It was great to have my daughter home for Thanksgiving. I only wish I got to see more of her. But I realized that she only had so much time and that it was important for her to connect with her friends.

PARENT REFLECTION

Monthly Checklist: Recommending Campus Resources

☑ Early October is a good time to remind your student about campus support systems. The way you recommend the use of academic and nonacademic resources may determine whether your child will actually seek them out. Personal counseling, academic advising, and tutorial services may be especially helpful at this time.

☑ Know something about the campus resource you are recommending. Refer to orientation notes or college literature.

☑ Encourage your student to take advantage of workshops in time management, test-taking strategies, and note taking. Student newspapers, bulletin boards, and web sites can be good sources of information for times and locations.

☑ Communicate your support. Discuss with your student the advantages of using a particular resource as part of his or her academic strategy.

☑ Encourage. Don't demand! Remember, it's all in how you say it.

☑ Place responsibility on your child for making the initial contact with a resource. If you make the call, your student may not feel compelled to follow through.

☑ Remember that campus resources are not just for resident students. Commuters should feel comfortable accessing these services as well.

Facing Finals, Family Holidays, and Semester Break

December and January

> First semester home I think I probably drove my parents crazy. I had adopted a completely new vocabulary and was spouting off about paradigm shifts and phallocentricity at the dinner table. I'm sure they wanted to strangle me.
>
> Student Reflection

Finals are over, the holidays are approaching, and semester break is here. You're looking forward to your son's or daughter's coming home, you've made some special plans, and you've arranged to spend some extra time with your college student. Your child arrives home with a very different agenda: eat, sleep, and spend time with friends. What's going on?

Holiday visits, and, in many cases, an extended break in December and January, can present challenges for the student and the rest of the family. A long break can be a source of great excitement *and* considerable tension. You and your child have survived the first semester of college (for better or for worse) and have survived the processes of problem solving and growth. Semester break provides an opportunity to reconnect, reflect, and rejuvenate.

DECEMBER and JANUARY ISSUES

Student Issues

1. I wish I could get home earlier so I could help prepare for the holidays.

2. I hope I stay healthy when I'm home. I hate colds and the flu. Winter always gets me down.

3. Final papers, final exams, final grades! I'm really feeling overwhelmed right now.

4. I need to be careful about dealing with stress. With Christmas parties and all, there is a lot of alcohol around.

5. I'm looking forward to seeing my friends during the break and comparing our college experiences.

6. I'm anxious about getting my first-semester grades. I hope I did well.

7. I may have to make some decisions about my major. I might even consider transferring.

Parent Issues

1. I hope I can deal with my child. There have been a lot of changes.

2. Planning for the holidays is not the same without everyone here.

3. I know my student needs to connect with friends during the break. I just hope we have some time to talk.

4. Semester grades will be coming. I'm a little anxious about how my child did.

Final Exams

For the first-year student, the end of the first semester can be a real milestone. For some, it represents a major, positive achievement. They've done well academically, coped well with all the changes in their new environment, and established new friendships. For others, the experience may not have been all that positive. Academically, they may have floundered, and their adjustment to their new environment and their peers may leave much to be desired. Now they may be finishing up last-minute details for required papers, as well as facing the prospect of dealing with their first set of final exams.

The majority of students face their first set of finals sometime in December, at the end of the first semester (final exams may take place earlier for students who are on a quarter system). It goes without saying that final exams can create their own unique stressors. Parents can play a key role in providing much-needed support and encouragement to their student at this time.

The exam schedule is usually posted well in advance of the end of classes. Once classes end, most colleges designate several days as a reading period, a time for students to prepare for exams. Organizing time in order to make the best use of this reading period is no easy task for first-year students. Many students with poor time management skills may inappropriately view this reading period as downtime and focus on socializing. Knowing how to prepare and how much time to devote to each subject can be a delicate balancing act. It can be especially tricky when a student has more than one exam scheduled on the same day. Students will find that the more organized they are in preparing for finals, the more confident they will be as they approach these exams.

> *Our daughter felt really overwhelmed during the last few weeks of classes. She had worked so hard during the semester, and now she was really struggling. She had two papers due and was concerned that her exam schedule was so tight. We encouraged her to set up a schedule for herself and break down larger tasks into smaller ones. We felt relieved when she called to let us know that she had joined a study group. It helped her to feel a little more in control.*
>
> PARENT REFLECTION

It is not unusual during exams for students to feel overwhelmed and run down. Staying up late, cramming for exams, consuming large amounts of caffeine, and eating on the run can result in physical and emotional fatigue. In fact, for many students, "pulling an all-nighter" can become more the norm than the exception. As a result, students run the risk of becoming physically ill at a time when they need to be healthy and in control.

Students can feel "stressed to the max," and they need to be careful how they deal with this stress. The desire to unwind and connect with their peers can contribute to excessive use of alcohol, which can interfere with their ability to function well. It is important for students to recognize that during this stressful time, they need to call on those internal (things they do to help themselves) and external (places and people) resources that have helped them cope in the past.

➤➤ Studying for college **finals** for the first time can be stressful for your student. Your son or daughter may need you as a sounding board. Just listening may be enough.

➤➤ Many colleges offer **tutorial programs** that provide special assistance during exam time. These resources can be reassuring and provide important direction for your child.

➤➤ Help your son or daughter to identify ways to **deal with stress**: exercise, sleep, and good nutrition. You might recommend that your child check with the college's personal counseling services for stress management tips and for assistance in fine-tuning his or her coping skills.

➤➤ Final exam time is cold and flu season. This additional stress can contribute to your student's feeling really run down. A visit to the **student health center** might be in order.

➤➤ This is a great time to send your child a **care package** from home. Notes of encouragement, snacks, and homemade baked goods are always appreciated.

Home for the Holidays

You are probably anticipating your child's return home from college as you eagerly await the hustle and bustle of the holiday season. It may represent a time of family traditions and gatherings. It may also be a time of considerable tension since it usually comes at the end of the first semester, after finals and just before semester grades.

By now, plans should already be in place for your child's return home. Be sure your student makes travel arrangements well in advance. If traveling by car, your son or daughter may be sharing a ride with a friend, or you may need to adjust your schedule so you can pick up your child. Also, find out how your child's personal property will be stored and secured at school while he or she is at home. For example, if storage space is limited, your student may decide to bring his or her computer or CD player home.

Your child's schedule is bound to have an effect on family holiday planning. How much it affects the holiday season depends on his or her previous role in the family as well as how important it is to both of you to uphold family traditions. The timing of some holiday rituals such as selecting and decorating a Christmas tree, purchasing Hanukkah gifts, or baking favorite dishes may need to be revised. For example, if your college student made sure that your house was always the first one on your street to be decorated, then that tradition may have to be changed since your child will not be home in time to do that. It might be important for you to discuss this issue with your child before the holidays so he or she will know what to expect. You might decide to delay the decorating, or, for practical reasons, you might go ahead with this activity in your child's absence.

COMMUTER SIDEBAR   This can be a time of mixed emotions for commuters. They are happy to see friends return home from college, but may feel left out when conversations shift to roommates and living away from home. Remind your child that everyone's experience is unique and that he or she has much to share.

As you prepare for the holidays, it is natural for you and your child to recall rituals and activities of past years. These familiar routines bring a sense of comfort and hominess to the occasion. Don't be surprised, however, if you also experience feelings of sadness and even a sense of emptiness as you realize that things are not quite the same this year.

Your son or daughter may also be experiencing some mixed emotions at this time. While your child may be caught up in the frenzy of end-of-semester papers and finals, he or she may occasionally daydream about past holidays with family and friends. Your child may look forward to the excitement of being home but also may be anxious about how the holiday season has changed.

> *We wanted everything to be perfect when our son came home, but it was hard to know what to do. We wanted to wait for him before we decorated the tree, but his little sister really wanted the tree up. We felt pulled in both directions. We called him at school to get a better sense of his expectations about the holidays. I think it helped to talk, since we were all a little uptight about some of the changes.*
>
> PARENT REFLECTION

Strategies for Parents

➡➡ **Be flexible**. You may have to postpone certain activities or develop new traditions to accommodate your college student's schedule.

➡➡ **Be realistic about expectations**. You may not be able to fit everything in this year.

➡➡ Although you may be full of **holiday plans**, don't be surprised if your child has little to contribute. This may be especially true if he or she has just completed a stressful week of finals. You may have to let your child set the pace.

Semester Break Challenges

How smoothly the first-semester adjustment process went can have a major impact on semester break. Your student may still have some concerns about academic performance, roommates, friends, choice of major, or just a general sense of fitting in. This can preoccupy your child's thoughts during the break. Most colleges post first-semester grades on the college's web site or mail them out shortly after the holidays. This may heighten anxiety during the holidays.

Parent and student expectations over grades may or may not be in sync. In other words, you may get some surprises if your child's vague responses about grades during the semester led you to believe that all was well. His or her performance may have been marginal. On the other hand, your student may have indicated that he or she was struggling academically and reached out for support. As a result, you may be sharing in your child's anxiety in the wait for grades. Of course, if your student informed you throughout the semester that things were going well academically, then this might be a time of happy anticipation and excitement.

Whether your child receives good news or bad news, your response can provide an opportunity for meaningful dialogue. It can also set the tone for second semester. If your student did well the first semester, you will want to validate his or her academic achievement and give encouragement to continue the good work. Remember that it is important for students to balance study time with extracurricular involvement. You may need to help your son or daughter deal with feelings of disappointment, embarrassment, and maybe even anger over grades. Students need to assess what factors contributed to their unsatisfactory grades, which may involve a discussion about study habits, time management, outside activities, and basic adjustment issues. The conversation may provide clues about nonacademic issues that might be interfering with your child's ability to do well. For example,

Semester Breaks

a difficult roommate situation may be preventing your student from getting sufficient sleep or having a negative impact on study time in the dorm room.

Although grades are an important issue, other academic issues may also surface. Your child may be questioning the choice of a major or feel pressured to choose a major soon. It could be a particularly delicate issue if he or she has done poorly in courses required for the major. Your student might even jump to the premature conclusion that the major is not a good fit and neither is the choice of a college.

Second-guessing decisions about the school, the major, or the courses can sometimes make parents and students look for other options. They might visit other schools and download transfer applications off the Internet. Some students might even consider taking time off and applying for a leave of absence from their college. Sometimes this can be healthy and even therapeutic, since students feel they have more options and more control of the situation. At other times, this decision can be counterproductive since it doesn't get to the root of the problem. In fact, it puts the focus on the school rather than on the student.

In a sense, the arrival of first-semester grades serves two important functions: it helps to put a feeling of closure on the first semester, and it provides an opportunity for parents and students to reevaluate what has occurred and what might be done differently. For example, now might be a good time to talk to your child about improving his or her test-taking strategies. A tutorial service can help your student with study skills, test anxiety, and time management. For the student who has had an ongoing roommate problem, you might help by identifying campus resources or individuals whom your child can seek out to help resolve the problems. A discussion about the amount of time spent socializing versus time devoted to course work might also be appropriate at this time.

> *We felt that our son really needed to get his priorities in order. His grades simply did not reflect his ability. We worked through our disappointment by helping him to review some of the choices he had made, such as not taking advantage of tutorials and allowing himself to become overextended by getting involved with too many activities. We helped him to brainstorm changes he needed to make. He had been elected freshman class president, and we were proud of him. But it was important that he realize that something else had to give.*
>
> PARENT REFLECTION

Even a student who has done well academically might still wonder if he or she is at the right college. Students who make only a few friends, participate in very few activities, and generally feel disconnected from the college may question whether they should return for second semester. This can be a fragile issue and requires your patience, support, and encouragement. You and your student may have to make some decisions about financial aid concerns, scholarship requirements, or athletic stipulations. Help your son or daughter work through feelings and explore possible options while still putting the responsibility on your child to make decisions.

How your child spends time during the winter break depends on the length of the break and other commitments. Some students spend all of their time relaxing, socializing, and going on trips with family or friends. Many students, however, spend this time working to make money for second semester. Some students start exploring summer job opportunities.

During the break, remember that for an entire semester, your child has been making personal choices and decisions: when to get up, when to go to class, and how late to stay out at night. Things obviously will be different at home. You may need to discuss your expectations with your child. You may be concerned about curfews, telephone, and money. For example, at school, your student may have been used to having friends call at 2:00 A.M. or spending time on the Internet well into the night. Now that your student is home, he or she may be totally unaware of how these behaviors disrupt the family routine.

> *When Christmas break came around, we expanded our son's curfew. He eventually came in when he wanted and turned off the hall light when he was in. So if I awoke, I would know he was safe if the light was off. If it was still on, it was my choice to worry or go back to sleep.*
>
> Parent Reflection

Your child's presence at home may also change the dynamics of the family. Of course, a lot depends on the size of your family and the nature of the relationships prior to your child's leaving for school. For example, a relationship with a younger brother may be different now. They may be spending more time together. In some cases, just the opposite might occur.

Some students take this opportunity to reconnect with people from their past such as former high school teachers, coaches, or guidance counselors. They may look forward to sharing their experiences, asking for advice, or just getting some validation that they are on the right track. Such meetings might be particularly important for students who have had difficulty making the transition from high school to college.

Strategies for Parents

➡ Although your child's overall adjustment to college may not have met your expectations, don't overreact. **First semester brings some unique challenges** that may take some time to resolve. Your encouragement and support are what is needed most.

➡ Parents should be aware of when final grades are available. Information can be found in the college bulletin or on the college web site. Keep in mind that each college has its own interpretation of FERPA, and therefore you may not receive **your own copy of your child's grades**.

➡ A student who has done poorly may be **reluctant to share grades**. If your child does not bring up the subject, make sure you do.

➡ Let your student know that you can help him or her brainstorm about options and develop a plan of action for **second semester**. Of course, the responsibility rests on your child for follow-through. It is important that he or she take responsibility for decisions.

➡ If your child's lack of commitment to academic work is reflected in his or her **grades**, you might feel both disappointed and angry. Although these feelings are legitimate, try to put them in perspective as you talk about your concerns.

➡ Keep in mind that your child may have to study during **break**. If exams take place after the holidays, he or she may have to study for finals. There may be an incomplete grade, and your child may need to finish some course work to receive course credit.

➡ At many colleges, **offices and services remain open** during the break. If there are some serious issues that need to be addressed when your student returns to school, suggest that he or she call and set up an appointment prior to returning to school.

Getting Ready for Second Semester

Your child's behavior during the final days of break may take on the same hectic pace as the few days before first semester began. The flurry of activities might include visiting relatives one last time, hanging out with friends, and doing some last-minute shopping. The difference, however, is that your child has completed a semester of college life and now has a record of performance. How well your student adjusted to the college environment, academically and socially, can significantly affect how he or she approaches the second semester.

A student who is feeling upbeat about the first semester probably will look forward to returning to school, getting involved with classes, and re-uniting with friends. If your student's expectations were not met either academically or socially, he or she may dread the thought of returning. Whatever the case, there may be situations that need to be reevaluated and require your child to set up a plan of action.

> *First semester I fell into the trap of going out every night. My grades suffered. I learned my lesson. I thought it was like high school and that I only had to study a little to get by. It is a lot different. I know I have to make changes when I go back.*
>
> STUDENT REFLECTION

Some students may have discussed issues of grades and social life with their parents early on during the break and then put them aside. For others, these conversations may have been continuous. Parents can be especially helpful at this time by encouraging their students to explore options and define realistic goals. The goals should be concrete, attainable, and focused on the ability of the student to assume responsibility for follow-through.

Academic goals might include reviewing study habits, considering a schedule adjustment, or deciding on a change of major. Action plans associated with these goals include setting up an appointment with tutorial services, contacting the registrar's office, or meeting with an academic adviser. There also might be some specific academic needs that may require a number of interventions. For example, if arrangements were made to have your child assessed for a possible learning disability, then test results need to be forwarded to the appropriate campus resource. A follow-up appointment should be scheduled to discuss possible accommodations.

Goals involving personal or social concerns might be to resolve a room-mate problem, rethink involvement in extracurricular activities, or reassess spending habits. Actions might include meeting with someone from residence life, expanding or limiting involvement in clubs or organizations, or setting up a more realistic budget. Certain behavioral patterns may require a combination of interventions. For example, if partying was more of a priority for your child than studying, he or she may need to connect with counseling services as well as tutorial services to get back on track.

Whether your student's first-semester experience was positive or negative, it's time now to get ready to return to school. Some students look forward to second semester with great anticipation. Although they may have some hesitations about saying good-bye to family and friends, they are eager to reconnect with their college friends. For others, saying good-bye is no easy task. Even if they may have good feelings about their college, it can be difficult to give up those familiar comforts of home.

Your emotional response to your student's departure may be quite similar to what happened at the beginning of first semester: conflicting feelings of sadness, loss, anxiety, pride, and excitement that resurface. For parents who have experienced some aspect of the empty-nest syndrome, their child's return to school may rekindle some of those same feelings. Knowing that these feelings are appropriate can help you cope with them in a way that will not interfere with the emotional responses of your college student.

Strategies for Parents

➧➧ Holiday blues, academic concerns, and difficulty saying good-bye can make **leaving for second semester** an emotional experience. This may be a time when students could use some extra TLC.

➧➧ It is okay for you to have **mixed feelings** about your child's returning to college. One way of coping is to acknowledge your feelings and, if necessary, talk them through.

➧➧ Don't be upset if your son or daughter is really excited about **going back to college**. An eagerness to return to friends and roommates is not necessarily a reflection of how your child feels about home.

➧➧ If the **first semester did not go well**, remind your son or daughter (and yourself) that all is not lost. Focus on the strengths, and brainstorm ways to regroup.

➧➧ **A successful first semester** is something to celebrate. Nevertheless, sometimes it can put more pressure on a student to keep up the high level of performance, or it can cause the student to get involved in too many extracurricular activities. A balance is important.

➧➧ When you discuss any **second-semester changes**, remember that your son or daughter "owns" the plan. Your role is to share your expectations and provide support, not to assume responsibility for decisions and follow-through. That is up to your college student.

➤➤ You may want to restate the importance of connecting with **campus support systems** — campus ministry, counseling, tutorial services, and others.

Monthly Checklist: Returning to School

☑ Make sure travel arrangements are in place well in advance.

☑ Double-check move-in dates and times for returning to the residence hall. If changes need to be made to your child's on-campus living situation, your child should make contact with the residence life office to confirm the new arrangements.

☑ Depending on the day your student returns, offices might not be open. If particular concerns need to be addressed, your child should call the appropriate office prior to returning.

☑ Be aware of important dates — the first day of classes and deadlines that may need to be met.

☑ Make sure that financial matters are in order. Billing issues or fee adjustments that need to be resolved can cause complications if they are not addressed in a timely manner.

7

Staying on Track

February, March, and April

> *Upon my arrival freshman year, I had my share of problems fitting in and making new friends. By the time I had returned second semester, I knew who my friends were, and I felt a real sense of belonging. Once spring break came along, I wanted to spend my vacation with these friends. I'm glad my parents allowed me to go away, because it helped me to develop a closer relationship with the people I now call my best friends.*
>
> FIRST-YEAR STUDENT

Whether the college is on a quarter system or a semester system, students may experience somewhat of a letdown after the holidays. February, March, and April bring practical and emotional challenges that may test your child's perseverance as well as your own patience. Readjusting to a new semester, registering for sophomore fall courses, and deciding on next year's housing can cause major stress at this time of year. Cabin fever and spring fever can play havoc on even the most organized and motivated student. Emotionally it can be a time of extreme highs and lows.

FEBRUARY, MARCH, APRIL ISSUES

Student Issues

1. I have to learn to readjust to new routines and a new course schedule.

2. I'm really missing my family and friends from home. I also miss some of my college friends who didn't return to school.

3. The weather really affects my mood. How will I cope with cabin fever, spring fever?

4. I really feel pressured to improve my grades this semester. I need to re-think my study skills to do well on my midsemester exams.

5. I hope I make the right decisions for next year. Who will I live with? What about my courses and my major?

6. I hope that I don't get the flu this winter. I am really going to try to exercise more and work on staying away from eating so much junk food.

7. How can I convince my parents to let me go away for spring break? Will I have enough money?

8. There are a lot of parties right now. I have great friends, but I sometimes feel pressured to drink.

9. I should start thinking about a summer job. I'll check things out during spring break.

Parent Issues

1. I know I have to adjust, but I really miss my child. It was great having my student home during the break.

2. I hope my student's grades will improve this semester. I need to make sure my expectations are realistic.

3. What if my child is sick this winter? How can I help? What about missed classes?

4. My child wants to go away with friends for spring break. We need to talk about some of my concerns before we make a decision.

5. Choosing a major is such a big decision. I hope that my child's academic adviser is helpful.

6. I wonder how my child is coping with course registration. I know choosing a major can be stressful.

● ●

Settling In

Once back on campus, students may find themselves facing some of the same challenges of first semester, but with the added demands of new classes and different professors. Getting back into the swing of campus life requires new routines, new course strategies, and renewed relationships with roommates and friends. For some students, this will be a smooth process. For others, it will be more unsettling and may call for a reevaluation of what did and did not work during the first semester.

Many students become concerned that some of the same feelings that they experienced during those first weeks in September have suddenly returned. Missing family, friends, and a comfortable environment can stir up those feelings of sadness and loss. It is important for students and parents to remember that the first-year adjustment to college is an ongoing process and to be aware of the ebbs and flows of the academic year. Realize that it involves a continuing series of progressions and regressions.

> *When I came back to school second semester, I felt as if I was beginning all over again. Although I had friends at college and liked my roommates, I really missed my family and my friends from home. I was a little embarrassed to tell anyone that I was feeling homesick. I felt better when my friend e-mailed me and told me he was feeling the same way. At least it wasn't just me.*
>
> STUDENT REFLECTION

It is typical for students to spend the first few weeks of the second semester connecting with one another and catching up on how they spent their break. Students may be surprised to find that not everyone returned. Some may have transferred to a different college. Sometimes a student takes time out due to personal concerns such as finances, family obligations, academic difficulties, or just a rethinking of priorities and goals. Whatever the reason for not returning is, the absence of a friend can be upsetting and can bring about feelings of profound sadness. It can even cause students to question their own decision to stay in school.

Reconnecting with roommates can have its ups and downs. Obviously students look forward to renewing relationships that flourished first semester. On the other hand, if the roommate situation was less than ideal, feelings of anxiety and resentment are bound to resurface. For students who have had a negative roommate experience, it is not unusual for them to come back to school intending to make things better. As a result, they may invest a good amount of energy on trying to create a less stressful living environment. For example, if a student continuously played loud music while a roommate was trying to study, the assistance of the resident assistant or hall director might be sought out to help establish new ground rules.

Academically, there may be considerable readjustments. Even students who did well first semester need to get back into a rhythm of studying and course preparation. Dealing with new course material and new professors with different styles of teaching presents some real challenges. Once again, time management issues take on a primary role. For example, the time schedule for classes may have changed significantly from last semester. A student who had all early morning classes may now have more classes scheduled during midafternoon or late in the day. The new schedule may require the student to adjust sleep and study habits.

Students who return to college in academic difficulty have a number of key issues to address. First, they must cope with the emotional fallout of their poor academic performance. At the same time, they are feeling pressured to improve, yet may not know how to go about it. Often these students feel that they are the only ones having difficulty, and they may feel isolated from their peers. These feelings can contribute to a student's withdrawal and interfere with his or her ability to create a positive plan for change.

COMMUTER SIDEBAR Parents need to be aware that second semester will bring a change of academic schedule for commuter students. Classes will be at different times, and routines will change, so work hours and transportation needs may have to be adjusted. Parents may want to lend some extra support to their commuter student who may be missing friends who have returned to college after the break.

Strategies for Parents

➡ Don't overreact **if homesickness issues resurface**. Think about how you helped your student cope last semester. Try to communicate your support and encouragement without letting your own anxieties take over.

➡ Just as your child may have some difficulty **getting back into the swing of things**, so might you. You may find yourself preoccupied with your student's readjustment. It is important that you reestablish family routines, especially if there are still siblings at home.

➡ Hopefully, you have already shared your **expectations for second semester** with your son or daughter. Allow your child some time to settle in and put plans in place. This can be especially difficult if there were problems the first semester. If you need a quick resolution to problems, you may interfere with his or her ability to assume responsibility and take action.

➡ If changes need to be made, remind your son or daughter what needs to be done and what appropriate actions need to be taken. Questions such as, "Who have you talked to, and what did they recommend?" can **encourage two-way communication**.

➡ Don't miss an opportunity to **encourage the use of resources**. Connecting with resources early in the semester provides necessary support and increases the possibility of meeting expectations.

Cabin Fever and Spring Fever

Spring Fever

🐚 *My parents sent me newspaper clippings about back home, notes of encouragement, and care packages. It really helped get me through the winter.*

STUDENT REFLECTION

The area of the country where your child attends college can have a direct impact on what issues he or she may be addressing at this time. For example, students who attend colleges in New England or the Midwest may find themselves dealing with cabin fever soon after they return from holiday break. Long winters and short days contribute to this emotional state. On the other hand, students attending college in the South or West may have symptoms of spring fever shortly after they return from break. All the sunshine and warmth make it difficult for them to spend time indoors. In either case, staying motivated and on track can be a difficult process.

Although some people find winter invigorating, the prolonged periods of cold weather and darkness can take its toll on students who live in a residence hall. Being confined to a small, closed-in environment can make them feel emotionally isolated, physically out of sorts, and, for some, depressed. Irritability and impatience with friends and roommates over minor issues can be a direct fallout of cabin fever. Combine this with midsemester exams, and your student's stress level increases greatly.

A small percentage of students engage in negative behaviors at this time. Many schools report increased incidents of vandalism, substance abuse, and physical or sexual assault during this period. Life becomes monotonous, and, unfortunately, a small number of students feel entitled to act out.

This can also be a demanding time for a student's physical well-being. The cold and flu season is in full swing. Living in tight quarters may make your child even more susceptible to illness. Your student may miss some classes, an added source of stress. Lack of activities or just plain boredom may find your child eating more junk food than usual and maybe putting on unwanted pounds. Lack of exercise can also contribute to students' feeling unhealthy and uncomfortable with themselves.

Parents may be particularly frustrated at this time. While trying to encourage and support their child, they may feel a sense of helplessness trying to help their student cope with the situation. You should not be surprised if you hear a lot of negative comments during these months. *I hate the food. I can't stand my roommates. My classes are boring.* These are all very typical complaints.

Worrying when your student is not healthy only complicates matters. Telephone calls from a sick student can be especially upsetting for a parent who is many miles away. Trying to determine how ill he or she is and what resources may be available can be a difficult assessment to make on the telephone.

> *Our daughter called home and said she was sick — sick enough to go to the infirmary, since she needed a note to defer an exam. This reminded me of when my other children called to say they were feeling bad and how they wanted me to come with chicken soup and take care of them. This can be a frustrating time for a parent.*
> PARENT REFLECTION

Although there may be some common elements with cabin fever, spring fever brings with it a whole new set of concerns. Lack of motivation may come as a result of continuous springtime distractions. Blooming flowers, bright blue skies, and a series of warm, sunny days can make it difficult for students to concentrate on course work. A desire to spend more time with outdoor activities can cause your child to procrastinate and put off important tasks.

> ੨♪ *It was really hard to keep focused. All the sunshine had me wishing
> I was outdoors throwing a Frisbee rather than having to study. I
> really needed to work on my concentration.*
>
> STUDENT REFLECTION

The social pace on college campuses picks up considerably in the
spring. Some students are heavily involved in sports and intramural programs. The number of on-campus organized events and unsanctioned off-
campus parties increases significantly. As a result, students tend to spend
more time gathering in groups and just hanging out. When common sense
and moderation rule, this can be a fun and enjoyable time. However, this
carefree and uplifting environment can sometimes lead students to make
unwise and careless decisions, especially regarding peer pressure. For example, a student who has decided to spend the weekend studying for a
midterm finally gives in to her roommates' pleas to go to an off-campus
party. Even though it is 1:00 A.M. and they have all been drinking, they decide to walk back to the campus in the mild spring weather. They may not
be in full control and therefore may be oblivious to the fact that they are
putting their safety at risk. Again, they may make themselves vulnerable to
physical or sexual assaults. Asking appropriate questions to find out where
and when your child is studying, what he or she does on weekends, and
how much money your child is spending and on what, can help parents get
a sense of how their child is coping at this time.

Spring Break

> ੨♪ *I opened up a credit card account to pay for my spring break trip to
> Florida. What a mistake!*
>
> STUDENT REFLECTION

Sometime during second semester, most college calendars include a spring
break, when classes are suspended for usually a week to ten days. Easter holiday or Passover may sometimes fall into this time period. Although some
colleges allow students to live in the residence halls during the break, many
schools require students to vacate their rooms during this period. Students
heading home for break may have made plans to work, secure summer jobs
or internships, catch up on schoolwork, visit friends, or just "chill out" for
a while.

While at home, some students have every minute scheduled. Catching up with friends can be a major priority. Just as during the winter holiday break, your son or daughter may spend less time with you than you had hoped. Your child may even invite a friend to come home with him or her, which may have an impact on the time spent with family. Although parents and siblings may look forward to this brief homecoming, they may be disappointed with the limited amount of time they have to share.

> ❧ *The real challenge during spring break was just getting to see our son. Although he was home, it was just a place to hang his hat — or in this case, laundry. He kept very busy with his old and new friends.*
>
> PARENT REFLECTION

Not all colleges are on spring break at the same time, so some students who go home may miss seeing their friends who attend different colleges with different schedules. As a result, parents shouldn't be surprised to hear their son or daughter complain about feeling bored and disappointed because they have no one to do anything with. Your child might even ask family members to rearrange their work schedules so they can spend time together.

Traditionally, this is a time when many students decide to take a spring break vacation with friends. It is not unusual for first-year students to get caught up in the flurry of the excitement of upperclass students who are making plans to fly off to exotic destinations for their spring break. If your child wants to take a vacation away from home with friends, you are obviously the best judge of the appropriate nature of this trip. If you feel strongly that your child should not go, be honest about your feelings, concerns, and possible fears. Depending on the situation, you might tell your child that you will discuss a spring break vacation again next year. If you are open to the possibility of such a trip in the second year of college, then be sure to talk about issues such as freedom, responsibility, money, alcohol, partying, and companions. You may want to consider the following strategies as part of this decision-making process.

Strategies for Parents

➼ Think about how your child has demonstrated **independence** and responsible decision making. How did your son or daughter meet the challenge? Has he or she traveled before without your supervision (perhaps on a high school trip)? Remembering these times can give you insight into your student's level of maturity.

➡ Knowing the **kind of trip** and whether there will be any adult supervision is obviously the first point to consider. For example, a trip to the Caribbean arranged by a travel agent is quite different from a trip to Appalachia that is sponsored by a campus community service organization. However, don't necessarily assume that a campus-sponsored trip is always supervised. You need to ask some very specific questions.

➡ **Ask how your child plans to finance the trip**. Is he or she paying the bill or assuming that you will cover or share the cost? Some credit card companies make their presence on campus prior to break to entice students to open an account. The temptation to use the card to finance the trip can result in your student's accumulating substantial debt, probably at a high interest rate.

➡ Do your homework. Ask questions about **safety and security issues**. Are the students staying in a remote area, an urban setting, or a self-contained resort? Will they be camping, hiking, or participating in riskier activities such as rock climbing or hang gliding? What is the legal drinking age where they will be going?

➡ Check out the **legitimacy** of those arranging the trip. Unfortunately, it is not unusual for inexperienced students to be taken in by companies and organizations that overcharge, overbook, and misrepresent services and accommodations.

➡ Be clear about your expectations. Concerns about **alcohol consumption, risky behavior, and personal safety** need to be discussed. Focus on the need for your child to be in control of self and surroundings.

➡ Depending on the destination, there may be concerns about what he or she eats and drinks. What provisions have been made **in the case of an emergency**? What are the medication needs and insurance coverage while your child is gone?

My daughter was invited to spend spring break with her roommate and her family. I was excited about her having a good time and bonding with her roommate, and I felt this really validated their friendship. I felt bad, though, because I missed her and really wanted to see her. I knew it would be a long time before I saw her again.

PARENT REFLECTION

Making Decisions

At this time of year, students usually face a number of decisions. Academically, they need to think about course selections for the following semester. Now that your student is more familiar with different teaching styles, chances are he or she will be concerned about which courses to take, as well as which professors are teaching them. For some students, there will also be decisions to be made about their choice of major. Some will be working toward deadlines to declare a major, while others may be thinking about changing their program of study.

Colleges have different policies as to when students must choose a major. For students who are still in the process of deciding on a major, there may be some additional steps they need to take before registering for sophomore classes. They should take advantage of meeting with an academic adviser or a peer adviser to discuss issues related to major, courses required to fulfill college requirements, and other options. They should also talk with professors who teach classes in their particular area of interest. Advising centers, career development offices, counseling services, and campus web sites are useful resources to students who are exploring majors, minors, and other programs.

For students who are considering a change of major, it is especially important that they make good use of resources. Students experiencing a lack of interest or poor academic performance in their chosen discipline may question their initial choice. Premature decision making without getting good advice may result in students' floundering with no clear direction. Leaving a much desired major because of poor academic performance can be traumatic. This is particularly true for someone who has had long-term career aspirations associated with a specific major. For example, a biology major who has dreamed of becoming a medical doctor since the fifth grade is having difficulty passing courses in chemistry and biology. He may internalize a deep sense of failure. Having shared his career goals through the years with family and friends, he may dread having to inform them of a change in major.

Parents can be supportive of their student by understanding his or her feelings. Communicating your support for future decisions can go a long way in helping your child overcome feelings of disappointment.

> *I was pretty certain I wanted to major in engineering, but after I got a D in my first Calculus 141 exam and a 7 out of 100 on my quiz, I really had to rethink my plans. My parents wanted me to continue down the engineering path, but they also encouraged me to*

talk with my adviser. He suggested that I drop the course. I started to focus my attention on my economics class, which really piqued my interest in business. Sophomore year I was accepted into the School of Management.

STUDENT REFLECTION

Choosing courses and making decisions about majors can be frustrating for first-year students. Taking the right course, fitting it in at the desired time, and selecting a specific professor are issues that can cause considerable anxiety. Parents can be very supportive during this time by helping their child put issues into perspective. Suggest that a large task be viewed as a series of smaller, achievable steps. Recommend that a backup plan be explored in the event that your student is not admitted to a competitive major. This backup plan can lower anxiety and reduce procrastination. More important, it can reassure your child that he or she is in control and can handle the task. Your encouragement will provide necessary support without taking away the responsibility from your son or daughter for making final decisions.

Nonacademic decisions may also need to be addressed at this time. For example, students living on campus need to think about whom they want to room with next semester, as well as where they will be living. They need to become familiar with the housing selection process: room lotteries, first-come-first-serve policies, squatters' rights. It is especially important that they meet any deadlines. Obviously the current roommate situation may dictate the kinds of decisions that your child makes. If there has been considerable conflict throughout the year, your student will want to live with someone else. Don't be surprised if your child wants to live with new friends even though his or her first-year situation has been positive. Sometimes current roommates may decide that they want different kinds of housing arrangements. For example, your son or daughter may want to remain in a single-sex residence hall, and his or her roommate may want to experience a coeducational living environment. Trying to work out these issues can be delicate and may cause them to go their separate ways. Allow your child the opportunity to work through these issues, seek early advice from the residence life staff, and take the responsibility for his or her decisions.

This is a time when decision-making skills are put to the test. The process includes gathering good information, discussing what was learned, generating possible options, weighing the risks, and making a plan. Some students are more vocal than others in discussing their decisions. They may feel that they have the situation under control. If your child does ask for feedback, you can be a good sounding board as he or she navigates through the process. But remember that the decision belongs to your child.

Strategies for Parents

▶▶ Don't be surprised if your child calls home complaining of cold or flu-like symptoms. Ask questions about symptoms and what he or she is doing to feel better. Refer back to orientation information concerning on-campus resources such as **student health** or the infirmary. If necessary, you might suggest that your child make an appointment with a doctor. Suggest that he or she check back with you after the doctor's appointment. If medication is prescribed, remind your son or daughter of the importance of abstaining from alcohol.

▶▶ Spring weather can trigger **allergies**. Know the resources available both on and off campus. If your student requires injections, be aware of treatment programs available and costs covered or not covered by student insurance or your own insurance.

▶▶ Most colleges have systems in place to assist students who may have to **miss classes or defer an exam** due to illness. Residence life staff can be especially helpful in referring your student to the appropriate office for assistance in this matter.

▶▶ If **motivation or boredom** is a problem, help your child generate possible solutions. Suggest that he or she get back into a routine, study with a group, get regular exercise, and use good time management skills. Remind your child to explore off-campus activities or special events that will provide a much-needed change of scenery.

▶▶ Your sensitivity and support can go a long way in helping your student get through the **winter blues**. This might be an especially good time to send a care package that is full of goodies, hometown newspaper clippings, money, and more.

▶▶ Remember to revisit values and expectations concerning **peer pressure and alcohol issues**. As outdoor activities increase, warn your child to take extra safety precautions. It is important for students to make good commonsense decisions, be aware of their surroundings, and practice self-control.

▶▶ Remind your child to use the **safety and security resources** such as campus escort systems and shuttle services.

Monthly Checklist: Keeping Them Motivated

☑ Send cards, e-mails, and little gifts on special days such as Valentine's Day, St. Patrick's Day, April Fool's Day, the first day of spring, and Easter or Passover. This parental thoughtfulness can be a great mood lifter.

☑ Sometimes a change in scenery can make a big difference. Encourage your student to consider a weekend home to regroup. Getting TLC from family and friends may be just what the doctor ordered.

☑ If necessary, revisit the need to make good use of campus resources. Tutorial services can help with concentration. This is normally a time when students frequently need counseling and health services. Students with cold and flu symptoms, allergy sufferers, and those experiencing the winter blues can especially benefit from these services.

8

My, How You've Grown!

May

> 🌺 *We need to allow first-year students the opportunity to grow. Tell them that you love them, trust them, and respect them. Give them the room to find new friends and the opportunity to discover the benefits of college life. My daughter has matured so much this past year. She is a different person from the one I left behind last fall. I can only hope she continues on this path.*
>
> PARENT OF A FIRST-YEAR COLLEGE STUDENT

The end of the first year of college is packed full of final exams, research papers, end-of-the-year activities, and final grades. Students who live on campus need to start thinking about packing up and moving out. Commuter students need to plan for changing their routine and reconnecting with friends who have been away at school.

By now, your student is looking for indicators that it has been a good year and that he or she has made a successful transition to college. A solid academic record is not the only indicator. Establishing relationships, coping with change, and taking risks are all indicators of a successful year. This chapter reinforces the idea that adjustment, change, and growth are ongoing. Transitions for parent and student will continue to unfold throughout the rest of the college experience.

> 🌺 *I can't believe that I've already finished my first year of college. Although at times it has been tough, I feel good about how I've coped with all the changes.*
>
> STUDENT REFLECTION

MAY ISSUES

Student Issues

1. I'm so stressed over finals, grades, and report cards.

2. It's going to be hard to leave all of my college friends.

3. I'm going to have to make some good money at a summer job in order to make enough money for next year.

4. How am I going to keep my independence living at home this summer?

5. I wonder which of my high school friends I'll connect with this summer? Will our friendship be the same?

6. I almost forgot that I have to pack up all my things and move out.

7. It's time to set some realistic summer goals. Should I go to summer school? Maybe I should go on a weight loss program. What kind of summer job do I want?

Parent Issues

1. Am I going to have to help my student pack up and move out?

2. I wonder how my child is coping with finals, research papers, grades, and report cards.

3. The family is going to be different when my college student comes home for the summer. I wonder if I'm prepared.

4. My child is getting a summer job near the college. I'm a little disappointed that my student won't be home for the summer.

5. I'm expecting my child to be more mature and independent. I hope my expectations aren't too high.

Preparing for Finals

The last month of the academic year is a time of significant stress and anxiety for first-year college students. Setting realistic priorities, knowing how to study, and managing emotions are major issues for students during this time. Meeting deadlines for final papers and projects contributes to the hectic pace. There are also many distractions that students face at the end of the semester. They may be preoccupied with thoughts of returning home, leaving new friends, or seeing old friends. These issues can interfere with your student's ability to focus and to stay on track.

Students who have experienced academic difficulty may view the last month of school as a way to salvage a low grade point average. But because so much depends on the outcome of final exams, a student's stress level may be at an all-time high. It can be a real challenge for students to keep their anxiety from interfering with their performance.

Having already experienced first-semester finals should give your student a better sense of what to expect. That experience may have helped your child get ready for this second round of testing. The end of the year is a good time for your child to reflect on what worked and what didn't work last semester. For example, rather than using the reading period as a time to socialize and sleep in, perhaps this time your student will realize that it is a crucial time to study for exams.

Your support and encouragement are very important during this stressful time for your child. Here are some strategies that can be especially helpful at the end of the academic year.

Strategies for Parents

➡ Remind your son or daughter how important it is to talk to professors about unclear or misunderstood material. Having sound information and extra help can give your child confidence as he or she prepares for **exams**.

➡ Reinforce the use of resources, especially **tutorial services**. Students should check on the availability of assistance early since heavy demand might limit these services.

➡ Encourage your student to stay focused. Exams need to be top priority. **Packing and moving out** can be put on hold for now.

➡ Focus on the **strengths and positive initiatives** that have helped your son or daughter get this far. Even though it may have been a difficult academic year, try to validate the positive.

Packing Up and Moving Out

> 🐚 *The end of the year was so hectic. I had to focus on exams and also think about packing everything up. I threw out a lot of stuff just so I wouldn't have to bother with it. It was hard to be organized. I just had too much to do and not enough time.*

STUDENT REFLECTION

Moving out

For most students, the end of the academic year brings with it the arduous task of packing up clothes, appliances, books, and other belongings to go home for the summer. Since students are preoccupied with final exams, parents often wonder when their child will get packed up and moved out. Information about deadlines, extra fees, and possible storage also needs to be addressed before your student leaves campus.

In the process of packing, your child may be surprised at the amount of stuff he or she has accumulated in a relatively short period of time. In some cases, your child may need to change transportation arrangements to accommodate the new possessions. For example, a student who had planned to share a ride home with a friend may find that it is impossible for both of their belongings to fit in one car. Some students have to consider other options, such as shipping items home, renting summer storage space, or renting a van or trailer.

Since most colleges do not provide storage facilities for personal belongings, storage arrangements should be made in advance. Many schools provide students with a list of local storage companies, but it is up to the student to make the contact and find out about the cost. To save on expenses, some students share off-campus storage facilities. Many companies pick up a student's belongings for free. To help the process along, students should have plenty of boxes for packing.

You and your student should familiarize yourselves with college regulations regarding the closing of rooms at the end of the semester. In order to avoid extra charges for cleanup beyond the normal wear and tear, your student should leave the room in much the same condition as it was back in September. If there are damages, a college usually bills students for damage costs and may even impose fines. Typically roommates, floormates, or all the residents in a building will split these damage costs. Most policies regarding these issues are in the student handbook or in a separate residence life information booklet.

Whether you have a direct or indirect role in your child's packing up and moving out, you might want to keep the following strategies in mind:

Strategies for Parents

➡ Remind your son or daughter to double-check the **moving-out** deadlines. Many colleges charge a fee for students who fail to move out on time.

➡ Caution your child to **hold on to graded papers, quizzes, and exams**. Saving computer files and disks is also a good idea. Your student may need this information later if there is a discrepancy with a final grade.

➤➤ Suggest that your child find out about any **clothing drive** campaigns on campus. Campus ministry, social work clubs, and organizations often collect leftover food, clothes, and furniture to give to those in need. This service can provide a useful way for your son or daughter to get rid of unwanted items and promote the social concern for others beyond the confines of the campus.

➤➤ Encourage your student to ask about the bookstore's policy on **buying back used books**. Although your child may want to keep many college books, there may be some that he or she may never use again, especially if they do not relate to his or her major.

➤➤ Recommend that your child take a quick look at where he or she will be living next semester. If your student will be in a **different residence hall**, it is a good idea for him or her to see the new accommodations, become familiar with the new surroundings, and plan for the future.

➤➤ Don't forget to update your child on any changes that he or she may encounter at home. **Share news** such as the loss of a pet or changes in the home environment. Some parents delay giving bad news so as not to interfere with finals and so forth. These things can be unsettling if they come as a surprise.

Putting Closure on the Academic Year

Final grades represent the accomplishments or failures of the first year of college and thus are the culmination of the academic year. They also provide closure to a time of major transition for both students and parents. Expectations and realities join together to have a considerable impact on a student's future academic career.

Students whose grades have met with their expectations can feel a sense of accomplishment and pride. They have worked hard, met their goals, and received the kind of positive feedback they had hoped for. They can look forward to their sophomore year with a solid record of academic achievement.

Other students may have had a more difficult time and received less favorable grades. Some may even find themselves facing academic probation or dismissal. These students may have some decisions to make during the summer months. For example, they might consider changing their major, taking a summer course for extra credit, or getting involved in a tutorial program.

It almost goes without saying that if your student's final grades are poor, you and your child will need to have a serious dialogue. This conversation can give your child an opportunity to reflect on the reasons for poor performance, explore ways of supplementing his or her academic record, and readjust future goals. Your son or daughter may even decide to take a leave of absence or withdraw from school altogether. Before making any critical decisions, your child should consult with the appropriate school officials. Most college bulletins or student handbooks provide names and telephone numbers of these individuals. Although parents may play a role in the decision-making process, it is your student who should make the final decision and follow up on any further action.

Some students may have difficulty putting closure on the academic year. For example, a student who has received an incomplete for a course will probably need to finish the course work within a designated period of time. A student who is dissatisfied with a grade may decide to investigate options for considering an appeal. In either case, the student should try to connect with the professor as soon as possible, since some faculty may not be available during the summer. If a student cannot reach a professor by telephone or in person, e-mail is often an excellent way to communicate.

Regardless of the outcome of final grades, your student may choose to supplement his or her education during the summer with extra courses or an internship experience. Such action can help to lighten a student's course load in the fall, enrich an academic program, or take care of deficiencies. An internship, which may provide a stipend or academic credit (or even both), can also serve to expose your student to a specific career field. Students should be cautious, however, when signing up for summer courses or internships. Although college policies may vary, most institutions require preapproval of summer classes. Students usually need to provide their college with a written description of the course they intend to take.

Whether for academic or nonacademic reasons, some students may consider transferring to another institution. Although this can be an appropriate move, careful consideration and planning can prevent further problems. Students who leave one college for another without putting closure on personal or academic problems may simply bring these same issues to another college. Transferring is not a quick fix. As a parent, you can help your child sort out the pros and cons of making a change.

> *Our daughter did very well academically, but she just didn't feel good about her college experience. She talked about wanting to transfer but was pretty vague. We let her know that we would support her decision but worried that she would regret her choice later.*

*We tried to help her get a better sense of why she was feeling the
way she was. She finally opened up to us one night and talked
about wanting to attend a smaller school that was closer to home.
She felt she was disappointing her dad by leaving his alma mater.
We carefully listened to her concerns and encouraged her to look at
all her options.*

PARENT REFLECTION

If your student is thinking about a transfer, he or she should find out as
much as possible about the other schools being considered. A campus visit
is highly recommended. Plan an interview with an admissions counselor
who works with transfer students to address issues about accepted credits,
housing availability, and scholarship or financial aid information.

At some point, parents also need to put closure on the academic year.
For some, this may not be an easy process. Although students need to take
responsibility for their successes and failures, many parents have "stock" in
their child's accomplishments. They have contributed personally and fi-
nancially to their student's first year of college. If grades have not met your
expectations, you may have to deal with your own feelings of disappointment. You may find it beneficial to work through your feelings before expressing your views to your child. Keep in mind that many nonacademic
adjustments and challenges may have affected your student's academic performance. Remember that in most cases, your student will have sufficient
time during the remainder of his or her undergraduate experience to improve an academic record.

*Our son had to change his major second semester, and as a result
he felt out of the loop with friends he was living with who were
still biology majors. He talked a lot about this over the summer.*

PARENT REFLECTION

Home for the Summer

Home for the summer usually means some major adjustments for students
as well as parents. Some of the changes you saw in your son or daughter
during semester break will now be evident in full-blown proportion.
Changes in appearance and behavior may seem more pronounced now that
your child will be home for a longer period of time. You may also find yourself less tolerant of behaviors that test the limits of your authority.

The first year of college brings many developmental challenges that focus on a student's need for identity, autonomy, and clarification of values. Some of the changes you observe in your child may be the result of his or her questioning former choices and family values. Be careful not to overreact. Many of these changes may simply be your child's temporary attempts to define self and separate from home and family.

Changes in appearance or personal habits may include weight loss or weight gain, different styles of clothing, language changes, new mannerisms, or altered eating and sleeping habits. Sometimes a student's search for identity can result in deliberate physical changes — some subtle and others not so subtle. For example, some students tattoo or pierce their bodies in order to express themselves. Other students may surprise their parents with bright blue hair or a shaved head.

Unfortunately, some students develop unhealthy lifestyle patterns while they are away at school. For example, a student's preoccupation with food may have intensified during the academic year. As a result, the student may return home with an eating disorder. For a parent, this can be a particularly difficult situation to address. Before confronting the issue, you should consult with a professional.

For some students, fake IDs, easy access to bars, and off-campus parties have become a way of life. Unless they have been penalized by college officials, they may continue these behaviors during the summer. If a student is engaging in risky behaviors such as excessive partying or illegal use of alcohol or drugs, parents need to take a strong stand.

Once your son or daughter returns home, it is important that you share your expectations regarding curfews, social activities, and family responsibilities. Pointing out the connection between behavior and its consequences can be an important step in redefining your role as a parent and your child's limits and boundaries. As you approach these issues, you may want to keep in mind that your student has changed and become more independent. As a result, you may need to adjust some of your own expectations. Early communication is especially important as your child attempts to connect with old friends. Since setting limits may be viewed as a threat to inde-

COMMUTER SIDEBAR　Parents of commuter students should be in tune with some of the emotional ups and downs their son or daughter may experience when friends come home from college. Excitement and enthusiasm about renewing old friendships may be affected by some of the changes in these friends. This change can enrich a relationship or, in some instances, make it difficult to reestablish old ties.

pendence and autonomy, you may find yourself caught off guard by the way your child responds to you. Clarity, consistency, and occasional compromise can go a long way in reestablishing common ground rules.

> *There was a real adjustment for all of us when our son first came home. We discovered that his nighttime activities began at 9:30 or 10:00 P.M. We were in two different time zones. We had to have some good conversations with him about being considerate toward other family members.*

> *Our daughter was more independent when she came home. We realized that we needed to make some compromises. We extended her curfew, but let her know that we still wanted her to call us if her plans changed. I think she appreciated our willingness to bend the rules as long as she continued to show consideration for our concerns.*
>
> PARENT REFLECTIONS

Your son or daughter may commit to a variety of activities during the summer: work, summer school, internship, volunteer experience, or travel. For some students, regaining a social life at home may be a major priority. During the first few weeks after your child comes home, you can expect a lot of his or her activities to be focused on social life with friends. Some relationships continue where they left off; others may never be the same again. Your child may also try to keep in touch with new college relationships. Expect constant e-mailing, telephoning, and even occasional visits with friends and roommates.

> *Support them in their choices. Guide them if necessary. Most of all, be patient. Be willing to let go of a child and welcome back an adult.*
>
> PARENT REFLECTION

Monthly Checklist: Planning for the Next Academic Year

The summer prior to the sophomore year can be a time for your son or daughter to consider some short-term goals for the next academic year. Signing up for summer courses, rethinking a major, readjusting his or her course schedule, and making plans with roommates are typical activities for the summer months. Your student may also begin thinking about some long-term goals such as planning for an internship or a semester abroad.

Once again, it is important for your child to take the responsibility for these decisions. As a parent, you can provide the necessary support during this process. You may also have some practical issues to consider at this time.

☑ Double-check financial obligations. Make sure paperwork has been completed for loans, payment plans, and scholarships. Final grades and academic credits earned can often have an impact on financial aid packages and scholarship renewals.

☑ Reconfirm the status of your student's insurance policy. If your child is covered through a separate college health policy, make sure it has been renewed. This is especially important for student athletes.

☑ If there is a possibility that your child has a learning disability that had not been diagnosed before, make arrangements for testing to take place during the summer. Confirm which office or college official should receive the documentation once testing is completed.

☑ If your student's goal is to spend a semester abroad, start planning well in advance. Information on requirements, courses, and finances can be gathered during the summer.

☑ Suggest that your child contact the appropriate college officials by phone or e-mail with any unanswered questions.

☑ If your student is living off campus next year, review what needs to be done: sign a lease, review safety issues, buy furniture, make travel arrangements to get to and from campus, or possibly clear the decision with campus officials.

☑ Be aware of the deadlines associated with your student's return to college in the fall. In some instances, airline or train reservations need to be made well in advance.

Appendix A: Learning the Language

Colleges and universities have their own technical language. In order to navigate the system, you need to become familiar with common college terms. This is particularly important if you are sending your son or daughter to college for the first time and may or may not have attended college yourself.

The following Glossary will help you become familiar with commonly used terms.

Academic calendar   Overview of a college's academic year, including semesters or quarters, recesses, important dates for final exams, class registration, and other deadlines.

Academic standing   Course hours completed and grade point average required for a specific year of college that is considered satisfactory progress.

Advising   The system responsible for helping a student to explore academic alternatives, choose courses, set goals, and identify appropriate referrals; can be provided by an individual.

AP (Advanced Placement)   Courses and exams taken during high school that may qualify for college credit. Decisions concerning course credit vary by institution.

Catalog   An official college document containing information about the institution, including degree requirements, curriculum, financial aid, faculty and administration, and campus resources.

Core curriculum   Usually refers to courses that all students are required to complete prior to graduation, regardless of their academic major.

Curriculum   Sequence of courses required to attain a specific degree.

Dean's List   Academic recognition granted for attaining a designated grade point average during a particular semester.

Department chairperson   A faculty member who serves as the administrator of an academic department. Some of the duties of this individual include overseeing scheduling and registration.

Distance learning   Providing learning through media (e.g., computer) where the teacher and student are physically separated.

Extracurricular activities   Term used to describe nonacademic, out-of-class activities that enhance a student's college experience — for example, social clubs, sports, and leadership experiences. Also referred to as *cocurricular.*

Faculty   Teachers at the college level who are usually referred to as professors. Levels of advancement and seniority are commonly denoted by the terms *full professor, associate, assistant, adjunct, guest lecturer, instructor,* and *teaching assistant.*

FERPA (Family Educational Rights and Privacy Act of 1974)   Refers to a student's right of privacy concerning release of information without authorized consent. Interpretation of this law may vary by institution. Also known as the Buckley Amendment.

Grade point average (GPA)   A grading system used to determine a student's status by a procedure of calculations. A grade for each course has a preassigned number of quality points, which are multiplied by the number of credits for that course. All the quality points are added together and divided by the number of credits. Schools vary on the number of quality points assigned to each grade.

Greek system   General term that refers to campus fraternities and sororities. Most local chapters are affiliated with a national organization.

Hall director (HD) or head resident (HR)   A full-time graduate student or professional who is responsible for overseeing the administration of on-campus living environment. This individual may also provide resource assistance to students.

Interdisciplinary   A course or academic program that consists of content or courses drawn from two or more disciplines.

Independent study   Opportunity for a student to participate in a project with a professor one-on-one. This experience is usually available to students in junior and senior years.

Internships and experiential education   A supervised work experience that exposes students to professional responsibilities in a career field of interest. Career planning offices at many colleges serve as a clearinghouse for internships. An internship can be paid, volunteer, or for academic credit.

Liberal arts   A broad overview of academic disciplines within the arts and sciences that includes languages, history, philosophy, art, and the natural sciences.

Living and learning   A special living environment intended to bring learning into the residence halls. Programs, which vary from campus to campus, might include faculty involvement in residence life, seminars, field trips, and discussion groups.

Major   Area of specialization consisting of a cluster of related courses drawn from one or more departments that usually requires a minimum of thirty credit hours.

Matriculation   Student is currently enrolled in and successfully making progress toward the completion of a degree.

Minor   A cluster of thematically related courses drawn from one or more departments — usually fifteen to eighteen credits.

Orientation   A program designed to introduce new students to the academic and nonacademic aspects of college life. Orientation usually takes place during the summer or just before classes begin in the fall. Many colleges now have a formal program for the parents of incoming students as well.

Placement tests   Exams given at the college to determine entering students' level of knowledge in specific subjects. Most common subjects are English, mathematics, and foreign languages.

Resident assistant or resident adviser (RA)   Student leaders who have been trained and reside in the residence halls. These individuals provide assistance and support to students on their floor. During the academic year, they coordinate special activities and programs for their students.

Student handbook   A college publication that provides students with basic information about college policies and procedures. Information on housing regulations, college resources, disciplinary procedures, and the student code of conduct are some common topics addressed in this handbook.

Study abroad   Receiving credit for course work while attending an institution in another country but still remaining a matriculating student at the original institution. Study abroad is usually completed in the junior year.

Syllabus   A course description including the requirement for the course, the student's responsibilities, and criteria for the final grade.

Transcripts   An official document that includes all of the student's academic courses, grades, credits, and academic status.

Undeclared/undecided   Students who have not yet declared a major. Many colleges have special advising programs to assist these students in their decision-making process that will lead to the selection of an academic major.

Appendix B: Campus Resources

Colleges provide a variety of services and resources to assist students. In order to take a proactive approach before problems arise, parents and students would benefit by familiarizing themselves with what each institution has to offer. When reviewing the resources that follow, it is important to keep in mind a number of issues. Although services may be similar in the kinds of assistance they offer to students, they may be referred to by different names at different institutions. In most cases, larger schools tend to provide more services.

Advising center   Central location for students to meet with academic advisers and receive information about course work and requirements. Individual or group advising may focus on choosing a major, supplementing academic programs, or making connections between a major and a career.

Billing/bursar/student payments   Office responsible for tuition, fees, and billings. May oversee payment plans and other related financial needs.

Campus ministry   Oversees the spiritual life of the campus community. Provides information about religious services, community involvement, spiritual advising, and counseling.

Career planning services   Designed to assist students with career exploration, self-assessment, internships, resumé writing, interview techniques, and all aspects of the postgraduation job search process. On-campus recruitment programs may also be available.

Counseling center/psychological services   Provides individual or group counseling to students experiencing personal and emotional difficulties. Services are confidential within legal and ethical guidelines. Unlike high school guidance programs, academic concerns are addressed by an academic adviser.

Dean's office   Functions of this office vary by institution. Deans may oversee student life, academic programs, or individual colleges. Some work more with students, while others may work more closely with faculty.

Financial aid office   Some of the areas this office oversees include federal work-study program, grants, loans, scholarships, and other forms of financial assistance. Provides information on eligibility, loan status, deadlines, and the application process.

Health services   Provides medical services and referrals. Some programs may be more comprehensive and provide full-time staff and facilities. A health education component may also be associated with this resource.

Learning assistance/tutorial services   Provides tutorial and study skills assistance. Tutors may be professional or trained students representing various disciplines. Services for students with physical or learning disabilities may also be coordinated through this resource.

Multicultural center   Responsible for planning multicultural programs and activities. May oversee a variety of cultural and ethnic clubs and organizations. Coordination of community resources and outreach activities might also be facilitated through this center.

Residence life office   Oversees all aspects of on-campus living, including housing selections, roommate assignments, and meal plans. This office may sponsor educational programs and outreach activities designed to foster community living within the residence halls.

Safety/security office   Responsible for the safety and security of the college community. Oversees parking regulations, crime prevention and awareness, and campus escort system. Campus crime statistics may also be available through this office.

Student activities   Office that coordinates cocurricular opportunities, including student activities and events, leadership development, orientation, and student organizations. May serve an advisory role to student government, fraternities and sororities, and the student newspaper.

Appendix C: Useful Web Sites for Parents

Alcohol and Drugs

http://www.whitehousedrugpolicy.gov

Current data on drug use, prevention, and treatment. Provides links to other valuable resources.

http://www.drugabuse.gov

National Institute on Drug Abuse comprehensive site addressing all aspects of drug use and abuse. Includes most current research.

http://www.college.health.org

A comprehensive guide to issues related to alcohol and drug use on college campuses.

http://www.clubdrugs.org

Provides information about "club" drugs. Consequences and symptoms are highlighted.

Financial Assistance

http://www.students.gov

Access America for Students, a federal government web site, provides access to government resources for planning and paying for education.

http://www.fafsa.ed.gov

The web site to file electronically a free application for federal student aid.

General Information for Parents

http://www.collegeparents.org

Home page of College Parents of America, a national association that provides important resource information to parents. Services, special discounts, and newsletters are available to members.

http://www.collegetownusa.com

Information for college students in general. Links to chat rooms, message boards, virtual college tours, and search engines.

Hazing

http://www.stophazing.org

Covers many aspects of hazing, including fraternity, sorority, and athletic issues. Information about antihazing laws, resources, books, and speakers.

Safety and Security

http://www.campussafety.org

Web site for Security On Campus (SOC), an organization geared specifically to the prevention of campus violence and other crimes. Links provide information about resources, crime statistics, and up-to-date federal legislation.

Bibliography

Americans with Disabilities Act (ADA) of 1990. Public Law 101-336.

Astin, A. W. "Student Involvement: A Developmental Theory for Higher Education." *Journal of College Student Personnel*, 25 (1984): 297–308.

College Parents of America. "College Parents of America Outlines Eight Points for Parents Speaking with Students About Alcohol." Available at: http://www.collegeparents.org (accessed May 18, 2001).

Family Education Rights and Privacy Act of 1974. *Congressional Record*, December 13, 1974, pp. 39858–39866.

Myers, E. Unpublished attrition research studies, St. Cloud State University, St. Cloud, Minn., 1981.

Perry, W. G., Jr. *Forms of Intellectual and Ethical Development in College*. New York: Holt, Rinehart & Winston, 1970.

Index

135

Notes

This is a place for you to record your own notes. If you would like to share your notes and your stories with the authors, you can contact them via College Survival by e-mailing **CollegeSurvival@hmco.com** or visiting our web site at http://college.hmco.com.